Deterring Wolves and Other Predators

A Rancher's Guide to Proactive Stewardship

MARK COATS

Deterring Wolves and Other Predators

A Rancher's Guide to Proactive Stewardship

MARK COATS

Kravitz & Sons
INNOVATORS IN PUBLISHING, MARKETING AND ADVERTISING

Kravitz and Sons LLC
204 E Arlington Blvd. Suite B
Greenville, NC 27858

Published by Kravitz and Sons LLC.

ISBN: 979-8-89639-628-4 (sc)
ISBN: 979-8-89639-627-7 (e)

Table of Contents

Acknowledgement I

Chapter 1 : Understanding the Principle 1

Chapter 2 : Selective Judgment....................................... 13

Chapter 3 : All or Nothing.. 22

Chapter 4 : Wolf Distribution and Microclimates 47

Chapter 5 : Predators... 54

Chapter 6 : Fear 75

Chapter 7 : Stockmanship 86

Chapter 8 : Dogmanship.. 122

Chapter 9 : Scenting.. 131

Chapter 10 : Monitoring.. 142

Chapter 11 : Conclusion 157

Training Cattle : Predator awareness................................ 160

Diagrams 177

Glossary 183

References 185

Comments And Observations 187

About The Author 189

ACKNOWLEDGEMENT

I would like to express my gratitude to Barbara March, Tammy Thompson as well as RB9 Publishing for their endless support and for their help in developing my writing skills. I would also like to Express my appreciation to Terry Miller for his help and support of setting up the website www.rancherpredatorawareness.com.

I would also like to thank California Cattlemen Association's Billy Gatlin and Kirk Wilber for answering endless questions as well as supporting my efforts.

I would also like to express my appreciation to Karin Vardamen and the California Wolf Group as well as Pam Flick with the Defenders of Wildlife. Their efforts provided me with many introductions, two of those introductions greatly shaped my understanding of the wolf. I would like to thank Carter Niemeyer and Tim Kaminski who enlightened me to many behavioral insights.

I would also like to thank Temple Grandin, University of Colorado, Ron Gill, Texas A&M Extension and Curt Pate, NCBA for their communications and responses over the years.

I would also like to thank Carisa Koopman Rivers whose brief stay as Siskiyou County Livestock Advisor helped me in understanding many of the human responses. I would like to mention and thank our new UCES Livestock Advisor Grace Woodmansee for her interest and helpful suggestions.

As to the general frustration and emotion that the wolf presents. Without the societal panic that this apex predator brings with it, my losses may have simply continued, rather than being addressed.

To the Ranchers who supported this endeavor, but due to that societal panic required an NDA (non-disclosure agreement) thank you for your participation.

To the person who made it all possible, I would like to thank my wife "Jody" for the never-ending miles, countless hours and for being the pillar of support throughout all the Challenges. Thank You and I Love You. Mark

To all of you, Thank You.

CHAPTER 1

Understanding the Principle

Predators are a risk to any ranching operation. The risk is not only depredations but the unsettled environment and the fear that the cattle are confronted with.

Losses can range from an actual deprivation to cattle being restricted from grazing. Daily routines, such as watering or seeking the best feed, can all be compromised. The harassment from a predator also affects the stock breeding and fertility. Not to mention the disposition and work ability of a set of cows.

Understanding the risks and the nature of predators is key to preventing losses of any kind.

Any predator requires specific behavioral actions to be successful in securing its prey. Each predator species has its own specific characteristics of hunting.

Just as domestic animals differ, such as a dog or a cat, so do wildlife. One thing they all have in common is that they all require an individual as prey.

Felines usually use the surprise tactic in securing their prey. Whereas canines are more apt to use the chase. Much like dogs chasing a car or a bicycle. The two predators differ in style, but both require the individual.

By working to stop the individualization of our stock, we present them with a comfortable "safe zone," which is the herd group. That grouping is nature's defensive posture for all herd animals. But through the years of management practices of separating without reuniting the herd, as well as no apex predators, our stock responses have weakened.

By promoting the *defensive posture of the herd group*, we rekindle a basic instinctual response to predators.

Once we promote and practice the *defensive posture of the herd group*, the stock soon seeks the group for comfort. The stock actively grazes within closer proximity to other stock, which I call *herd awareness*. This posture provides quick access to the *defensive posture of the herd group*.

Many deterrents focus specifically on the predators. Our focus is on our stock.

Although many deterrents engage the predators, that in itself is their drawback—by repeatedly engaging you risk desensitizing the predators. It's not much different from working with a young colt. The more time you spend with the colt, the more comfortable the colt becomes. The more contact the predators receive, the more comfortable they become.

All animals are governed by instinct. Fear is a response. It is summoned from the instinct of self-preservation.

If we understand that predators as well as domestic animals have instincts, we can begin to understand the basics of engaging an instinctual response and why it's an effective deterrent, whether it's our stock or the predators.

Another concept is animal communications. The animal kingdom communicates threw posture and scent. If you have been around a domestic dog going for his walk in the city, you understand his effort of marking his territory. You're also aware that the same dog is constantly sniffing and smelling as it seeks other markings left by others.

The awareness that scent is important to all animals, gives us an understanding of how predators mark their territory. This scent recognition offers another solution as a deterrent.

If we place a strange and unfamiliar scent, that scent will create a concern and an uneasiness. That uneasiness will engage an instinctual response, engaging a response of fear.

By placing a scent marker high in the breeze, we establish uncertainty. The inability to understand brings forward fear and its response of fight or flight. With nothing to fight, we are simply deterring presence.

Previously Instilled Behavior

Whether it's human or animal, established behavioral patterns are a challenge to change. Whether you call them habits, addictions, or established problem behaviors, they fall into the same category of being a formable pattern of behavior that is difficult to try to redirect. Preferably, such patterns would be avoided if possible, but often those challenges could already have been established, such as in wild-life and predators.

Such as a young preadolescent wolf from a known pack that has a long list of livestock depredations, such as the Rogue Pack in Southern Oregon. The short history lessons show that the individual has a high probability of moving south into California into a vacant and unoccupied area.

Possibly establishing a new territory, bringing with it a preset pattern of problem behavioral tendencies of preying on livestock.

The human behavioral tendency is to put off the challenge of the wolf because there has never been a history of a problem here. "There just aren't any wolves around here."

Many say that the wolves' presence is often related to elk, so you hear the responses of California just doesn't have a probable prey base to support the wolf, so an individual is most likely to leave the area rather than set up a pack domain.

Through my research, I often heard how adaptable the wolf is. I was told by a rancher in Washington State that a pack was on the coast and would swim out to sea and raid seal rookeries and then swim back for fresh water. Seals and elk have nothing in common. The only commonality is they're both prey victims.

California's varied climates and terrains, from sea level to its alpine peaks, present a prime habitat for such an adaptable predator. With its endless roads and agricultural endeavors and human populations along with their pets, it all presents a sizable list of opportunities.

When the reintroduction of the wolf began, I had the same response about the release of wolves over eight hundred miles from me in Yellowstone National Park. Yellowstone is just too far away to affect me.

The truth is, California presents a prime habitat for the wolves. The entire state is well within the wolves' travel patterns, making their presence just a matter of time.

The human response is also predictable. Some will confront the issue with fear and impending doom; others will attack the threat. Some will certainly promote bureaucratic and paper regulations although I realize that it's just hearsay. But I don't believe that predators can read. Others will change their perceptions and manage their instilled behavioral tendencies and adapt and become proactive stewards.

The reason for the telling of these stockmanship skills and presenting a response in our stock is to prevent predatory encounters. By instilling these proactive solutions, we have had a successful outcome in deterring losses to all predators.

Personal Interactions

Sometimes I'm asked, How do you know this? I'm always at a bit of a loss for a reply. My thought is to say, "Don't you?" But my rearing tells me that would be rude. I believe it's like turning on the TV or the radio. I don't understand it enough to repair it. But I certainly can use either the radio or the TV to my satisfaction.

I believe it comes down to a person's own interactions with animals and others.

The concept of our interactions affecting others is nothing new. It's just that some have greater responses than others. Whether those responses are negative or positive, their personal interactions are just that—they're personal interactions.

Oftentimes, when we are presented with challenges in our lives, those challenges are what shape our character. I am a believer that those challenges and how you receive them and your response are what establish your quality of life. The quality of life isn't based on the easy way, but rather your effort in dealing with those challenges.

A leader that believes he must rule by having others submit to his ideas is certainly a militaristic approach. But out of the confines of the military, it isn't a very effective action. That "do as I say" direction often finds its way into our interactions with animals as well as people.

Whether you choose words such as collaboration or partnerships, the name tag simply states it's a combined effort to reach a satisfactory goal. I believe this holds true for people as well as working relationships with animals.

Often, the challenge is swaying a preconditioned ideal or a preconditioned response. Depending on the depth of such established conditioning, such behavioral tendencies may have become too established to redirect. This applies to people as well as to the animal kingdom.

An Animals Response

As to the animals, it should be our objective to understand an animal's behavioral characteristics as well as species' behavioral tendencies. By making the effort to "work with" rather than "do as I say," we submit a successful conclusion to each engagement and begin a *working partnership* with whatever animal we are addressing.

When I say a *working partnership*, I am not suggesting that every animal will have a lapdog relationship but rather an understanding that we will interact with the animal in a way that satisfies and meets our objectives.

I believe this is why low-stress stockmanship was developed.

In addressing wildlife and our interactions there, I believe that *predator awareness* has been shown to effectively mitigate our risks. Through this understanding of our interactions with animals, we can start to realize and notice some repetition of responses and actions. After some time, we become comfortable with the idea that if I present myself this way, the animal's reaction will be this.

Wildlife is different from our domestic stock, the difference is in their ability to detect our presence quicker than we notice theirs. Their heightened sensory perception establishes the need to engage them while we are hidden or better yet not even there.

I realize that an animal's response may be one that is unintended, but most often, the response will fall into predictable behavior. Otherwise, any trainer or stockmanship demonstration would not be relevant or effective and we realize that trainers and stockmen are certainly relevant and needed.

I believe over the years and continued effort of trial and error, as well as learning from some admirable mentors, my understanding certainly is not complete but maybe slightly advanced over some others.

Any animal has a *thought-of-the-moment* response. The animal kingdom doesn't ponder what's happening tomorrow. Their actions and interactions are very responsive and reactionary rather than analytical. That is not intended to discount the ability of animals to shape their routines to a daily schedule or an animal being aware of your requests for specific pressures and responses.

Take a dairy cow who is milked at a certain time each day; often, that cow is waiting for the milker to lighten her load so she can get back to her job of eating.

Cattle that are in a set grazing rotation, such as a savory system, will have a similar response when they're routinely moved to fresh pastures.

Both of these examples of an animal's ability to learn and establish a routine, such routines are well within the predator's behavioral characteristics. These established routines should concern us as to the relationship between our stock and the predators.

Once the predators routinely patrol our stock, it is only a matter of time before the predators engage them. Once a reward has been achieved, a return is probable, and the first steps to an established pattern have been taken.

The natural world gives living creatures an understanding of their required needs, through the cravings of thirst or hunger. Those are powerful things. Although they are linked to sustaining life, they don't overpower the instinct of self-preservation.

Animal behavioralists may contradict this conclusion, but for hunger to overpower the *fear* of death, the animal must be in an extremely deprived state. In that case, the power of hunger may overrule the instinct of *self-preservation* as simple compliance.

Hunger engages movement. That movement is the act of searching for an opportunity.

Our stock can become the same opportunity as any established food source, if we present them as an opportunity to the predators.

By engaging the predators on an instinctual level, we engage a reaction rather than an action. First by presenting a deterrent that addresses the presence and, second, by instilling a response by training our stock to seek a *defensive posture* rather than the response of *fear*.

I realize to many that are watching a lion stealthily stalking its prey, one could perceive that it's engaging in an analytical thought process in its approach. My conclusion is that the predator is responding to opportunity and relies on its instinctual stealth tactics to acquire that prey.

But outside of established routines, the animal kingdom is reactionary. Whether the response is stopping or moving, either action is generated by some perceived or well-understood pressure or stimulus. When we address *stockmanship* and the reactions to specific pressures, when those pressure and releases are practiced, they become an established response quickly.

The method of applying specific pressures and then releasing those pressures instantly when the proper response has been shown by the stock. This sets to memory for the stock, a solution for the relief to such pressures. This pressure and release create a *trainable moment*, which establishes a response to similar future encounters.

To the predators, our applied pressure is to its heightened sensory perception and presenting an unknown which draws forth a *low-level fear*. That unknown will also cause a response. The relief to that unknown pressure will be to leave the area.

I often hear, well, what about eating and grazing, which creates movement? Exactly, the grazing movement is from the stimulus of hunger. Just as the response of flight is a response to the instinct of *self-preservation*, which has *generated fear* as a means of avoiding any *perceived threat*.

By overcoming *fear* for our stock, we intervene in the absence and present a comfortable solution for our stock.

As to the predators, we present a couple of situations that bring forward an instinctual response.

Instincts

Instincts have a stronger engaging action than anything we can present to the predators as a deterrent. Those *instinctual responses* such as *fear,* is a manageable tool that engages responses instantly. By incorporating *instincts* into deterring presence, we remove ourselves from having to encounter the predators personally and can simply present a nonunderstandable unknown, which engages the *instinct of self-preservation*.

This engagement of the predator is simply applying a stimulus that will generate a predictable response. That response is that it will draw out an instinctual reaction.

By instilling a response and a solution to a perceived threat we subvert an instinctual response from our stock of flight or fight. That response of *fear* is then replaced with a comfortable and secure posture. That posture is the *defensive posture of the herd group* and the *standing solution*.

The animal kingdom is based on responses to *perceived pressures*. Whatever the response or action is based on the animal's perception of that moment. This is why *pressure point pressure* is an effective method of managing movement.

By effectively engaging an animal quietly and methodically, the animals are engaged in a *low-stress* method, effectively managing the animal's movement and desired outcome or destination. Whereas an abrupt and chasing method of handling brings forward stress that could be quickly elevated to *fear*, as it draws on a response of the *instinct* of self-preservation.

By inserting the *relief of applied pressure*, we reward the proper response that we are seeking. That relief should come as quickly as possible and be left alone (*not repeating the exercise*) for a period. That rest will set to memory the proper response.

Without a break, an understanding of such *relief* will never come to the animal, and the animal will continue to seek other solutions for relief from those pressures. A repetitive training session only satisfies our personal objectives rather than the goal of establishing a desired response.

Whether working with our stock and promoting low-stress stockmanship, or whether it's removing movement for the training of the standing solution, when the relief to applied pressure is given, it's important to give enough dwell time to set to memory those proper responses. It's the stockman's choice of the moment to choose the required method.

Our interactions, if thought out, are more successful when we make the effort to understand our actions rather than forcing a submission from our stock.

To the predators and our interactions, there should be an understanding that their responses are purely *instinctual*. By engaging them on an *instinctual level*, we limit the predator's options, only leaving a response rather than an action.

By engaging both sides of a possible confrontation, the stock and the predators, we present and establish a solution of responses to such an engagement. Hopefully, our *interactions* are presenting a *"work with"* scenario rather than a *"do as I say"* command, which effectively obtains the desired response that suits our needs.

Efforts

I realize that time is valuable. The chores that need to be done on a ranch are never-ending. To me, it seems as if everyone is ahead of the game, and I'm always behind.

The truth is boredom on a ranch is only for guests and outsiders rather than the ones drawing wages or making a living there.

If predators are a financial concern or a problem, the method of *predator awareness* can be effective, but the process requires time and effort.

I happened to be at a meeting the other day, and a discussion arose about the accuracy of a specific concealed carry firearm.

This person was commenting on this concealed carry firearm and its inaccuracies. Several of us in this conversation actually pack this weapon when we're riding, simply because of its affordability and size.

When I started questioning this person about their conclusions about this weapon's accuracy, I realized that the person had made a minimal effort toward practice and becoming familiar with the weapon, laying the blame on the weapon rather than their abilities.

Any time that success is the outcome, that success was only a result of *effort*.

I have had this discussion throughout my lifetime, and there have been many responses such as what about winning at gambling. My response has always been, "You mean ranching?"

Whether it's gambling or ranching, you are still required to make an effort, whether it's purchasing a ticket, placing a bet, or building a fence. A successful conclusion requires effort.

Predator awareness isn't any different. A successful outcome requires an effort.

CHAPTER 2

Selective Judgment

I have come to realize that human behavior, as well as the animal kingdom's behaviors, haven't really progressed. Oh, things may modernize, and technology certainly advances and the quest to do away with the old ways certainly resembles progress. But in fact, that behavior is a steadfast characteristic of humanity. It seems as if the secrets of the past are unveiled and are represented as new discoveries. We just venture down a path that has already been well-traveled.

The saying about learning history is so you can avoid previous mistakes, but it only reflects on short-term American or European history and those historical events that are briefly acknowledged. But studying the circumstances that proceeded and created those major events takes an effort in study to understand. Often, the simple daily tasks just fade into the lost memories of times past.

The loss of understanding of history is only the result of humanity's quest for progressive innovations and leaving the "old ways" behind.

My great-grandfather fought in the American Civil War. My father told me the stories he was told by his grandfather when he was a boy. My father also told me stories of what he saw in China before WWII and in the South Pacific during the war.

My father often relayed to me that the war affected many people, and each individual remembered their own personal experiences.

His opinion of recorded history was it was simply opinions slanted by politics or social bias rather than the personal experiences or the conflicts of the social dynamics that set the stage for war. I believe such a record of history to be *selective judgment*.

This social shaping of recorded history is not new although, today, it's called cancel culture. They both refer to the same mechanics of rewriting history.

I make this qualification to history and human behavior to understand that human behavior really doesn't change through the chapters of time. In understanding human behavior, we can then look to the animal kingdom and realize they have none of humanity's quests for progress. Their quest is simply survival and procreation.

We as humans apply our personal emotions of fear, desire, happiness, or love to whatever animal we choose. But in fact, those are only our implied desires. The animals only have their instincts and their species' *behavioral characteristics*. If we interact with these animals and become an accepted occurrence within their environment, we as humans must apply our desires of acceptance to the animals to qualify our own personal self-esteem.

I realize that domestic species that become entwined into our daily lives and our affections for those relationships are real and an important part of each of our lives. My point is rather to the animals of the wild kingdom and our interactions there. We may become an accepted or a tolerated presence within their world, but anything such as affection is only a description that we ourselves put forward. Although humans believe that forgetting the past is part of accepting the future, that itself is just an emotional desire. The past is a fact, wishing it away or trying to forget it, or trying to change how it's reported doesn't change anything that had happened in the past. But an understanding of how history is recorded is also an important part of the question of what did we do prior to today to cope with specific issues such as predators. Although important to those who directly dealt with those predatory pressures, their efforts certainly didn't survive the historical recordings through time.

Historically, solutions may have taken a more direct approach, such as eliminating the problem. But modern times have brought forward protections for these predators. Living within these laws and regulations is where we are today. Making a social and economic statement to ranchers that the predators are here to stay.

Understanding that a lion then was the same in behavioral characteristics as a lion now is understanding that change and progression is only a human qualification to humanity, not in any way connected to the animal kingdom.

I often hear comments from research or qualified experts attesting to animal behavior and then the qualifying of the qualified. That same progressive objective is to eliminate history and rediscover a trail that has already been ventured down. I'm definitely not one who opposes academia but rather opposes academia's automatic disqualification of historical data to just hearsay and then an effort to replace it with their own study or data—only to qualify a more politically correct view or satisfy a more sustainable donor or an economical benefit to a system of higher learning, which they then charge and profit from.

Individualized research is a valuable study. It's unfortunate that the studies don't unite with one another with a "common sense" conclusion, tying the multiple papers into a theory.

As a point, I would ask how many studies must be done to understand gravity. Sir Isaac Newton was hit on the head by an apple, and he called it *gravity*. Yet when one university does a study on predators, it's like a sale at a discount store. Everyone just gets in line for their own variation of the same story.

Unfortunately, a study requires measurable statistics, which is why we see so many studies on the effects of presence and how the predators affect the cattle and the predator's economic impacts. If you deter predators from the presence, you don't have anything to measure. How do you measure a nonevent?

As to deterrents, it's easy to measure or physically see or understand that this apparatus should scare an animal. So let's walk this domestic animal past this apparatus and see if he has a reaction. Yep, he looked at it and seemed wary of it. Unfortunately, there's no way to measure fear, no gauge or measuring device, only our perceptions. That makes for pretty poor data research.

So I understand that the research must be to measurable impacts. But there is a measurable study that could be performed that would show how effective deterring presence is. But it would be a massive costly study of tracking with GPS, and the results of such a study may impact someone's operation adversely. The effects would probably generate another problem, which might be the legal storm it would set into motion.

So let me again state that all research is valuable, and we need more understanding of *fear* and *fear's response*.

With that said, I understand that for some, my efforts are simply hearsay. That is true. But throughout my life, I have witnessed innovative ranchers and their *horsemanship skills, stockmanship, environmental improvements*, or their *talents with dogs* become the basis for industry standards and avenues of research that have followed. I certainly don't put myself in the likes of such mentors but rather point out that fear and its responses, as well as instinctual reactions or nature's own postures. All those are certainly not a new concept.

To the environment, there are few changes other than the humans managing to insert their specific projects or to encroach, enhance, or manage it the way they perceive it should be. The animal kingdom throughout history has shown a unique way of adapting to the urbanization of our landscapes.

Predators require very little when it comes to basic needs, food, and water. Suburban areas present many opportunities for predators, and rural areas add their own assets into the mix. A predator's main requirement is water and prey. Water has stood the test of time, whereas prey happens to be the occurrence of opportunity. Even if there is historical data that shows a predator's preference for a specific game species, I will say that predators are opportunists. They will successfully adapt and capitalize on any situation that presents an opportunity.

Some history and traditions remain, but the reasoning behind why those traditions exist is lost to historical records. My first thought of such a tradition goes to the Alps of Switzerland and Germany. The belling of cattle has been passed down through the generations. The shapes and tones of these bells are specific and are actually called Swiss bells. Although they served a purpose of locating the grazing stock, my experiences and investigations lead to the conclusion that they were a combination of purposes of which one was also being a predatory deterrent. A traditional solution that survived the test of time for no other reason than the bell itself.

When you research past deterrents, you realize that deterrents present themselves into categories. There are deterrents that are intended to *frighten* or *scare* the intended. Such as a scarecrow in a garden, a blasting pop cannon, fladry, or radio playing loud music, fox lights or motion detectors, and a few more, I'm sure. These physical scare apparatuses certainly are effectively short-term, such as a trip through a haunted house for humans, but repeated encounters only see the original fear fade with the repetition of the apparatus's performance.

These apparatuses are only a tool for desensitizing and promoting habituation.

Then there are the *physical confrontations*, such as hazing or guardian animals, such as burros, llamas, or dogs. These interactions are intended to intimidate or confront a predator's pressures. Sadly, the predators being apex predators soon turn the table on guardians, and the guardians could soon be recategorized as victims. If the encounter is not lethal, it certainly requires medical attention. As to the hazing, it only sets an understanding of how far you are willing or able to pursue the predator, setting a finite understanding of the effort of the pursuit and your limits.

Another limiting factor to hazing or guardians is that both are better suited for small acreage than large ranges. The amount of guardian animals to effectively deter a large range brings added costs to feed and check on as well as veterinary costs, as well as the cost of the guardians themselves. It also requires added labor to routinely check how things are going.

Then there is structure, such as fencing the predators out or night corralling the stock in. Both are effective if plausible, but the cost factor often restricts the use of such deterrents.

Increasing predator populations and efforts to protect and reestablish predators that have been removed from the landscape has presented challenges to the livestock industry.

The public's misconception of the *ranching community* being flush with cash is a true misconception. Most years, ranching is about surviving economically and making the cash flow fit the challenges. Managing costs are the reason behind making the effort in deterring a predator's presence in the first place. That *mother cow*, as well as her *calf*, have costs incurred throughout their lives. That calves' sale is how the rancher makes his return. A predatory loss is not only about the animal's value but their incurred investment costs to date. A predatory loss only compounds the losses to future costs and returns. The mother's replacement will take a minimum of three years to replace.

Not only incurring the development costs of the new mother but the losses attributed to the lost mother's productive years as well.

Then there is *behavioral science*. As I stated before, humans qualify their feelings and place those characteristics onto animals. I believe that those human assertions rather than an understanding of the *animal's behavioral tendencies* are a major problem in deterring predator versus livestock conflicts.

By understanding that all living creatures have an instinctual base to survive, which is the *self-preservation* instinct. Then by realizing what *fear* is, it then becomes the key to understanding a basic fact of a deterrent. By understanding that relation of *fear* we can then use those *skills* to place or instill into our stock an effective deterrent. The *herd group* itself challenges the predators by not presenting an individual that the predators can exploit. Through years of reduced predator populations and stockmanship efforts of individualizing for management practices, our stock has become accustomed to being separated from the herd group.

An effort to reinstall the *defensive herd posture* as a deterrent is a very specialized task. Such training is not well-suited to be performed with other management chores. In our daily management routines, we have a purpose and a goal for our efforts.

Making an effort to have no movement is a self-defeating thought for some. I realize to many it relates effort to nonproductive results, kinda like a person who spends a lot of time on the couch. But as with first responders who practice situations, they may or may not ever encounter. Such training has the purpose of preparing for the chance of "just in case."

By making a concerted effort between the stock and *pseudo-predators*, we can reestablish such a response that includes the *standing solution*. By interrupting the *chase sequence*, we interrupt the predator-prey relation and promote the *defensive posture of the herd group*, which is an effective management solution in mitigating the risks of predatory pressures.

When we look at *behavioral tendencies*, some things stand out for all the predatory species. Predators could be described as elusive. That elusive nature is more of *instinctual self-preservation* than a learned behavior. Again, we see that instinct of *self-preservation* shedding light on an opportunity to deter presence. This acknowledgment of such elusiveness should not be just a brief mention but, rather, the beginning chapter in a book of understanding *fear*.

When we understand that *behavioral characteristics* and *instinctual responses* are different, we can understand why an applied deterrent will succeed. By engaging a response of *fear*, which all the deterrents present in the beginning, we engage *fear's instinctual responses of fight or flight*. Whereas *behavioral* actions are calm engaging action, such as stalking, which is an action rather than a reaction.

The key to success and remaining a successful deterrent is if the predators can't figure out what the deterrent is or if the deterrent manages to keep the predators bewildered. Challenging their *self-preservation instinct* and engaging an *instinctual reaction*. By not repeating an action, the deterrent presents an unsolvable uneasiness that keeps the instinctual responses engaged.

By presenting a repeating function, that function only acts as a desensitizing device. Not only not engaging an instinctual response after a short time of repetition but promoting a level of comfort in understanding the actuality of the nonthreat.

I believe when people listen to theories about predators versus stock, there is always a preconceived opinion whether it's proor antipredator. That opinion often sets the stage for a heated debate on what response to their presence should be taken, directing the conversation away from solutions and redirecting it to opposing the other side's opinions, leaving behind the thought of "how do we succeed in discouraging these encounters," and just debating and contesting the other sides opinions.

As I had said, I believe that human behavior directs actions of social bias and opinions rather than relying on the historical data. Following the *old ways* is just not *progressive* enough for societal evaluation. Even though those *old ways* and *nature's* own solutions, such as the *herd group* were historically effective in preventing predators from preying on livestock. Social bias discounts the effectiveness of the success to advance the *progressive agenda* to leave the past behind. Once again, I believe this to be *selective judgment.*

CHAPTER 3

All or Nothing

I don't believe that there are many *all-or-nothing* events in one's life. I believe that most of the time, it's about achieving an objective rather than this is the only way, or else, mentality.

By objectively seeking results to reach the desired outcome, you truly have to focus on what you really want to achieve. Too often, our objective gets entangled in emotional desires. I don't like *this (fill in the blank)* so the efforts become *doing away with "this"* rather than the effort of reaching the desired outcome.

The Frustration That Comes with Predators

As a rancher, I am concerned about predators and how they affect my bottom line. A ranching business is just that, a business. It survives or goes broke. My efforts must be to tending my business for it to be successful.

The ranching business is about production. It requires producing a product. For my operation, that product is a healthy, marketable, weaned calf; and having enough of those calves to cover the year's expenses, cost of living, reinvestment, and hopefully a profit.

With all that said, I must interject there's also the *quality of life* in the equation. Enjoying what you do is as important as earning one's wage, possibly of greater importance to many than one might think.

Often, if we don't like something, that dislike may frustrate or even anger us. But our reaction is based on it being a threat to our enjoyable *quality of life*.

The emotion of frustration or anger brings forward *instinctual responses* just as in all creatures. The *fear of losing our quality of life* brings *fear's* responses, *flight or fight*. Humans don't usually run away from challenges. That's why you often hear politicians say, "*We will fight!*"

When that frustration is directed at predators, we certainly hear the responses of shoot shovel and shut up. That is a reaction to the perception of the predators threatening our *quality of life*.

The threat or what that solution presents is that we place our objective of being a successful ranching business on hold while we engage this frustration of chasing this threat to our *quality of life* down a never-ending maze of illusions.

I do believe that it is a maze of illusions because when I was a boy shooting coyotes, it was just part of the way things were done. You looked for the gratification of hearing "good shot" rather than you pulled it or any other helpful suggestions. Although it certainly helped me become confident and comfortable with firearms. The entire effort was certainly ineffective in deterring any long-term problems that the coyote presented.

I am sure that over the years, the coyote population has not decreased, but rather, the population has gained in numbers. Making the effort of eradication over the years to be just a moot point.

The reason I call it a maze of illusions is our eradication efforts seems to have only perpetuated the coyote's numbers. So the time and effort would have been better spent on trying to present a deterrent. I believe that to be true with another canine species, *Canis lupus*, the timber wolf.

By chasing and concentrating on the wolf, what that presents to our *quality of life* is that we set ourselves up for a perpetual revolving door. That fills our time and robs the ranch of its required dedication. A better solution may be tending our stock more frequently and discouraging a predator's presence and developing new stockmanship skills that could deter predatory pressures. Such efforts promote our objective of tending and protecting the ranch and the *quality of life* we enjoy while promoting a profitable bottom line.

Seeking an Answer to the Question—What Can I Do?

It has been ten years since the famous wolf OR-7 first crossed my ranch in 2011. At the time, I would routinely lose five calves a year to predators. I felt as many did that I needed to confront the wolf because I certainly couldn't survive any more losses than I was already suffering. So the research began.

Since beginning my efforts, I have only had one loss in ten years. My efforts stopped the five losses per year, and that's a gain of forty-nine calves to my bottom line.

I had worked in a lot of the west. So I contacted those I knew who were dealing with the wolf, and a lot were dealing with grizzlies too. Most told me the laws needed to change. Waiting on Congress to change the ESA (Endangered Species Act) didn't seem to be much of a solution to me, as I had been witness to the devastation that the spotted owl had done to the logging industry and witnessed the deaf ears, their complaints had fallen on.

If you're an agricultural producer, you understand that only 2 percent of Americans are agricultural producers. If you're a rancher, you are of a much smaller percentage.

Our representatives have to take all their constituents into consideration. The simple math shows who will win when it comes to predator versus rancher laws or changing the existing regulations.

Simply stated, I don't believe that change will happen until public opinion demands such action. I don't see that direction changing soon. The ranchers will have to adapt to the increasing predatory populations and their pressures.

I believe that there are effective measures to mitigate the risks that the predators present.

If you look at areas where ranchers operate in wolf populated ranges, you'll find that often the same rancher is often repeatedly suffering losses. Yet neighboring ranchers within the wolves' range (approximately a fifty-mile radius) suffer no losses. That fact brings up an honest question, Why?

Were the wolves more interested in certain stock? Possibly, but the stock might have responded favorably to the wolves' tactics of separating and individualizing, making them an easier prey victim.

Possibly, stockmanship practices of separating for management and not developing a herd posture may set up a good opportunity for the wolves or possibly no use of stock dogs or even only using dogs that promote movement from rear pressure or even those that chase the stock.

Through the years of reduced predator populations and management practices of spreading the stock out and management practices of separating and no effort to reuniting the herd posture, we possibly could have set ourselves up in promoting our stock as easy prey.

A Wolf Workshop

In my research and one of many wolf workshops I attended, Dr. John Williams from OSU Extension Services did a presentation on collared wolves and collared cows that were both collared with proximity collars. When they got close to each other, the collar pinged to the GPS and gave the position of the stock as well as the wolves where those positions were recorded. The wolves chased the stock around a pasture all night and were only interrupted by human presence in the mourning.

I asked Dr. Williams if there was depredation? He said no, but the cattle were extremely flighty and had lost a lot of weight. He then discussed how the wolves costed the rancher in ancillary costs even without depredation.

I then asked if the rancher used dogs. His response was yes, but the cows who had been continually worked with dogs no longer could be, as they only sought to chase the dogs.

Several things jumped at me after seeing the presentation. Wildlife in my experience only exists for two reasons *survival and procreation.* That's it. They don't worry about the rent or what they're doing this weekend or anything that humans occupy their time with.

Several times, the wolves stopped to rest, even sometimes to regroup as if to discuss another scenario of attack.

The wolves' frustration just jumped off the screen for me and yelled, *Darn! What do we have to do to get an individual to separate?*

Any predator does not work all night for an empty stomach. Their efforts went unrewarded as they could not create or develop an individualized *chase sequence.*

I believe that's when I realized that for the wolf it is an *all-or-nothing game of survival.* Their requirement is that they must have an individual to exploit. The cattle being accustomed to being worked, moved, and handled by dogs instilled some previous training to remain grouped within the herd.

The wolves still pushed and herded those cattle all night. Although the cattle were still harassed all night and herded for many miles, their stock dog awareness probably help to mitigate the risk of an individual loss.

The wolf, in my opinion, would have continued the effort to secure its objective of a meal, if not for being interrupted by the human presence the next morning. The herding action never engaged any individualizations, and the wolves continued their pressure seeking such an opportunity. Their intent was a 100 percent focus on the objective. An *all-or-nothing* effort.

A Solution Begins to Form

Prior to this event, I had taken in a set of very spoiled cows to winter for another rancher. Our location requires feeding cattle through the winter, and these cows would just mob the hay wagon, actually injuring some cows in front that were mashed into the wagon from the pressure of the other cows trying to get their chance at a mouthful of hay.

I had been given a pup from a neighbor about a year before, and this pup showed a lot of promise in becoming a very good stock dog, but controlling his slow or stop was challenging for me. So I started to use him on this spoiled set of cows. Soon, that pup had these spoiled cows waiting to come to hay until I called the young dog off for a release of pressure for the cows. The cows would then walk to hay in a calm manner.

The young dog was developing, but after the cows were eating, he still wanted to work. At the time, I was trying to slow him down rather than stop him, but soon, he would have the cows tightly bunched into a group again, driven off their hay.

My efforts of slowing this young dog never did happen, but my solution at that point was after the cows were eating, I would put the dog in the cab of the pickup. I believed at the time that it would constitute a break in his momentum, allowing my wife and I to finish feeding these cows.

Then one day, after the young pup was put in the pickup and we were feeding the second or third trip of hay to the cows, the cows stopped eating and grouped together on a hillside, my response was that the pup must have gotten out of the pickup!

Before ever seeing the pup, I was yelling for him. The pickup was obscured from our vision, but my calling never brought the pup. When we got back, the young dog was in the truck, waiting patiently for our return. Why the cows grouped was still a mystery to us.

As time passed and these spoiled cows became well-mannered, they soon began calving. Our property is next to the Klamath Basin Wildlife Refuge, so coyotes have always been an issue here during calving season.

On one routine day, we were feeding our second round and counting calves when the cows stopped eating and grouped again. This time, I just sat. No yelling. Just wondering what was going on. As we watched the cow's attention, they directed our attention to the refuge and through the brush and onto the county road walked a group of coyotes.

I hadn't realized until that moment that the pup and his efforts had reestablished the stock's instinctual response to the *defensive posture of the herd group*.

Predators of All Species

I contacted and spoke to many animal behavior experts. They all seemed interested but were cautious in their responses. One told me to watch more actions of predators online to see if I could relate my theory to such a response.

What I found was an amazing fact for all predators. Whether it was African lions and the Cape buffalo in Africa or wolves in Yellowstone preying on elk, each and every predator required an individual to be the prey. Even as many would say the predators would just learn to attack the herd group, the only thing I could see is every time they approached a herd group, the effort was always to find an individual and exploit that individual's weakness. Searching and individualizing the weakest link, the herd group itself was each time a successful deterrent to predation.

Behavioral Tendencies

Through my research, I posed the question to many, Are there *behavioral characteristics* that are *behavioral tendencies* within a species, such as male canines lifting their leg to urinate or as females requiring a more seated posture?

Could one pose such a question that there are *behavioral characteristics* to each species? In most cases, I was told that *behavioral characteristics* could apply within and across each species.

Just as male dogs lift their legs or feline bury their scat, *behavioral tendencies* can present some insight into a predator's predatory actions. With all the predators, we realize they require an individual to become an individualized prey participant and that the herd group is an effective *defensive posture.*

The Requirement of the Chase Sequence

When we look at the species of canines, we can look at our domestic dog's problematic actions, such as chasing bicycles or chasing a car passing by. Those *behavioral tendencies* could be applied across the species.

The chase that the domestic dogs are uncontrollably drawn into is a baseline *behavioral characteristic* of the *canine species. The chase* has nothing to do with hunger nor anger or pleasure. It is purely a *behavioral characteristic of canines.*

Granted that predators that apply *the chase sequence* effectively, probably (more often than not) eat what they were chasing. But understanding that a dog chases a car because of *behavioral tendencies* gives us an understanding of how important the *chase sequence* is to the canine species.

As to the car, if it's parked, does the car initiate a response, or does the dog try to eat that same car? The answer is no. The movement of the car or whatever the object is, that movement is the stimulus that engages the response of the pursuit or engages the *chase sequence.*

Interrupting the Chase Sequence as a Deterrent

Through my studies, I have determined that *movement is intentional.* As to the stock, such movements could be to pressures, from weather, predatory, perceived, or to such tasks as grazing or watering. By removing movement and instilling a reaction of seeking other stock for the *protection of the herd group*, you could instill a response into a reaction, which I called the *standing solution.*

By developing a response to outside pressures, such as predatory pressures and promoting a response of the *defensive posture of the herd group*, you interrupt the individualization that the wolf must have. Then by removing movement and instilling a response of the *standing solution*, we interrupt the stimulus that engages a *predatory behavioral characteristic*.

Why Does This Solution of the Herd and the Standing Solution Work?

Through my research, I watch many hours of videos of every type of predator and prey. Those videos don't pose any research. They are only historical events that captured a moment in time and were recorded. I believe they are themselves historical evidence.

The predator's requirements and the prey victims had consistent relevance in all the engagements.

The reason for the deterring effect is the *defensive posture of the herd group* presents a challenge to the wolves' instinct of *self-preservation*. The challenge that a *herd posture* presents is a low-level *fear*. That *fear* engages *instinctual responses* rather than a thought process. Those responses are *fight or flight*. The *standing solution* itself doesn't present the movement that engages the species' behavioral characteristic of the *chase sequence*.

The combination has proved to me and my bottom line to be an effective deterrent. By engaging instinctual responses rather than predatory efforts, we change a predator's actions from an *all-or-nothing* event to a nonoccurrence or just a *nothing*.

How to Develop the Defensive Posture

You could then look to other sights online, such as stock dog training. What you may see often is trainers using a set of sheep or goats in a confined area to start a young pup. The trainers would carry a staff, stock flag, or cane. The staff is their tool to interrupt the pup when it becomes too aggressive. The sheep or goats soon learn that the safest place to be is right with the trainer or the shepherd. That response is an instinctual herd posture. The shepherd just happens to be the anchor or the lead or support of that interaction.

Many cow dog training videos showed a dog's ability to stop and group a set of cattle into a herd posture. The cattle's response was a defensive stance against the dog's engagements. The dog's actions removed the response of flight.

One thing that was noticeable and dissimilar was the speed of the dogs and the stocks response, which was quite different from those responses and herding techniques of a well-trained stock dog.

The well-trained stock dog promoted movement with a stealthy, calm quality that engages movement by the direction of the handler, not promoting an aggressive action or creating any *fear* within the stock— an action of being an extension of the stockman and his decisions of what were the proper movements.

Whereas the young pups, or some might call *overly aggressive* stock dogs, promoted by their speed, created an instinctual response of *fear* in the stock.

That *fear* then began the process of *desensitization*, which removes movement, engaging the *defensive posture of the herd group* and promoting the *standing solution*.

This response of removing movement is the same response as desensitizing a young horse at the beginning of creating a working partnership that will endure for the horse's lifetime. This desensitizing or "sacking out" removes movement and engages a calmness.

The "sacking out" creates *fear*, but with a steady rhythm, the horse soon becomes accustomed to the effort. This action of desensitizing works on all animals, it removes *fear* and replaces it with calm resolve.

The speed and lack of stealth was the only difference in action between the young pups and the overly aggressive stock dogs versus the quality stock dogs. The stock dogs manage the stock's movement from the direction of the handler, whereas the pups or the overly aggressive stock dogs only created *fear* and *desensitization*.

For the reason of defining the difference between a well-trained stock dog and a dog that presented a perceived threat to the stock. I called the stock dogs just that—stock dogs.

I then applied the name *pseudo-predators* to the dogs that invoked *fear* in the stock. Their speed and stopping ability engaged the instinctual responses of *fear* in the stock.

The response to *fear* is fight or flight. But as herd animals are herd animals because of predators, one might say that *fear* has yet a third response for herd animals, and that is the *defensive posture of the herd group*. Such grouping of the herd if developed further instills a calm and safe place for the stock, promoting and enhancing the *standing solution*.

By practicing for the desired response from our stock, we instill an effective response. If a predator should present itself, when we are not there, the stock's reaction will be to repeat and recall an already-instilled reaction to such predatory pressures.

We should not leave the training of our stock to any predator. Rather, we should instill our training to replace our stock's *fear* and give them a calm resolve to meet the goal of deterring those predatory pressures.

That calm resolve will transfer the *fear* away from the stock and present the *fear* back to the predators, engaging the *self-preservation instinct* and a sense of uneasiness for the predators.

Other Deterrents

When I was searching for answers to my questions about the wolf, I would listen to anyone who would give me a response. I was the local cattlemen's president at the time and was receiving many questions from other ranchers about the same questions I had. What can I do?

The wolf here in California and Oregon is still protected by the state's ESA law, and I believe it will continue to be protected for quite a ways into the future although the USFWS delisted the wolf federally, effectively limiting our actions as ranchers in California and Western Oregon to only using nonlethal deterrents.

I spent a lot of time reviewing and learning about nonlethal deterrents from people who had an underlying objective. I'm definitely not saying they were misrepresenting their intent but rather saying they may have been misinformed about what they perceived to be facts.

I had contacted some state representatives who gave me phone numbers of contacts for several NGOs. I contacted most of them but only had two that responded. I had a great desire to understand wolf behavior, pack dynamics, and their social structure. Often, I found that their perceptions were as jaded as the antiwolf group. Somewhere in the middle lay the truth.

I began working with Defenders of Wildlife and The California Wolf Group, trying to create a Range Riders Group as a deterrent. The intent was to develop a solution to mitigate the risk on large tracts of land such as forestry permits.

The concept was to keep the cattle together as a herd group and move them routinely to a new grazing area. The human presence and the scent left by that presence would itself act as a deterrent when the range riders were absent.

The Range's Intentional Design

The problem was that a herd group can only be maintained as a herd group if there is enough adequate water to water the entire herd group at one time. Being a high desert, the water source, or lack of, became a problem. The range's water supplies, depending on the daily heat index temperatures, could only water around thirty head per visit, disrupting the herd and spreading them out once again.

Some of the water sources were pumped to sixteen-foot water troughs. That one trough watered approximately two hundred pair (two hundred mothers and their calves). Certainly, the cows all had their allotted time to water. That water allotment time was the determining factor in how big a herd group would be.

That herd group size was also the determining factor for training for the *defensive posture of the herd group.*

The minimal water supply had small groups of cattle watering and heading back out to their specific grazing locations. As the cows who just watered headed back out, they would pass another set, approaching and coming into the water.

The allotted time was consistent. If you saw something such as an individual calf that required attention, you could return the next day at the same time and find that same calf and that same group of cows it was with watering.

The original intention in the development of the range was to spread the grazing out evenly. The lack of apex predators and the thought that they would never return added to the reasoning of spreading the stock out as truly beneficial to the range's design.

That fact and design make keeping the entire herd as a group an unattainable solution.

Although the herd group is often thought of as one's entire inventory, the naturally occurring herd size, determined by water availability, defines the required herd count and develops a *defensive herd posture* much better than one's entire herd.

The watering and history, as well as the forage supply, dictate what a trainable herd group should be for a specific range. The forest permits that I assisted on had groups of twelve to fifteen pairs per group. I would say a minimal group size should be at least three pairs. Training should focus on your range's specific needs.

The Deterrent Strategy Must Fit

If your supply of water is adequate enough and feed is abundant, your predatory defense may fit the range rider scenario better than the high desert conditions we have here.

Many promote solutions such as apparatuses that scare or frighten the predators. That action without a true challenge is just a deterrent for a minimal length of time. Each repetition without consequences only acts as a desensitizing device.

By desensitizing the predator, you present a calmness, which is awareness, that this apparatus is nothing to *fear*, promoting a comfortable and secure place to remain.

There are many who believe that confronting the predators, such as hazing or with guard animals, is a viable solution. It possibly could be in smaller areas, but on forestry permits or large pastures, those solutions pose other problems of much-needed additional labor and added expenses. I believe that fladry also falls in that labor and expense column as well.

Activists versus Active Stewardship

One might ask, If these deterrents aren't effective, then why do they promote them? My apologies if that is your interpretation. They do have strong historical data that supports their claims when they are applied in their optimum setting.

My experiences are on larger pastures and ranges in tough countries. In those cases, the labor costs exceed the estimated losses that the wolves would create, making the deterrent more costly than the losses. Then if the deterrent can't cover the rugged country, the chance of a loss still exists, only compounding the economic injuries to the ranching operation.

Often, many that promote a solution don't understand the vastness of the environment or the ruggedness of the terrain that these cattle work in. Often, these areas have no fences or roads and only contain the cattle by the geological parameters.

I worked with a wildlife biologist for a while, and he always said, "The wolves are about people." It didn't sink in. In the beginning, it actually took a few years and a few experiences to understand his statement.

Many activists who would be considered pro-wolf are blatantly antirancher, and most ranchers that would be considered antiwolf are actually anti-activists. I believe that both sides fall into that *all-or nothing* mindset and lose sight of the objective.

The activists, in my experience, present solutions filled with emotional reactions that often oppose some faction of human behavior that they don't like. I'll relate the efforts to protect the spotted owl. Many believe the activists' agenda was dismantling the logging industry. They may have promoted the owls' protection, but the consequences were the destruction of the logging industry and the devastation of the owls' habitat.

By eliminating sound forestry management practices, the forests have become inhabitable tinderboxes—not suitable for the owl and promoting the largest forest fires that are actually consuming towns and human lives, actually destroying any and all habitat.

Trying to develop effective solutions is proactivism, such solutions must focus on the animals rather than opposing other people that you don't agree with.

There are some who believe the solution will be found within an agency or bureaucracy and regulations placed on people rather than developing a proactive response and the interaction between animals.

In my opinion, the solution must be a solution that's about the predators and their interactions with the stock.

Communicating with the Predators

The animal kingdom communicates through posture and scent. Human understanding often relates communicating as speech. Although vocal engagements are certainly within the animal's community, scent would be one that humans have difficulty in understanding.

We understand that a bloodhound can follow a specific scent trail because of the hound's heightened awareness. That sensory perception within the animal kingdom is just unimaginable to humans.

Understanding that predators mark their territory by scent, in an effort to avoid confrontation with other predators. They're stating to the others, "This is mine." That gives us an understanding that if we could present a scent to mark our territory, there is some evidence to prove that it would be an effective deterrent.

It is also important to remember that by presenting a deterrent, we cannot simply desensitize the predator. The scent must engage a basic *instinctual response*, drawing on *instinct* rather than an understanding of a nonthreat. That nonunderstanding must draw a response from the *self-preservation instinct*. That nonunderstanding could be described as confusion or a grade of low-level *fear*, engaging an *instinctual response* from *fear* that responses are fight or flight, and since there is nothing to fight, the response is to move on—successfully deterring presence.

In order to continually present an ever-changing scent that the predator will not become accustomed to, we must continually present a new scent. These scents need to be powerful and in no way connected to the natural environment we present them in.

In my experience, if we present a solution that engages the desired response, that response is the deterrent. Through my research, it was often asked, "Well, can you prove it works?"

The question was often related to scenting, as I would have those who would say that driving around drinking beer was an effective scent deterrent. It's not. Human scent and their accompanying scents are completely understandable to all predators.

What I needed to prove to myself was that a scent could deter presence.

The Scent Test

In order to qualify the scent as an effective deterrent, I placed a trail camera in an area of an abandoned forestry allotment that had plenty of signs and tracks of multiple species of predators. The placement required seclusion. No human interactions or cross contamination of any other scent.

I checked this camera several times throughout a month's time, and there were occasional photos of wildlife passing by as well as some predators.

After about a month, I placed an attractant and aimed a camera at it. I secured the attractant by wiring it to a small tree. The attractant was a road-killed skunk as they are abundant and plentiful in our area and are a very good predatory attractant.

Just to let you know, no matter how careful you are when dealing with dead skunks, there are certain consequences. My test wasn't one of my wife's favorite things to show her support for.

This test site or camera trap was located on the east side of a ridge that divides the Shasta and Butte Valley. The ridge and its multiple peaks are often called by specific areas, but it is generally called Goosenest Ridge.

I set up this test site and monitored the daily wind and its direction. I didn't measure the velocity but ventured a guess of five to ten miles per hour of a breeze each afternoon. The breeze was consistent in coming from a westerly to southwesterly direction.

In monitoring the camera trap, I would check it every ten to fourteen days. I would ride in at midday to make the best effort so as not to encounter any wildlife. I would pull the chip and replace it with another as well as monitor the batteries.

I would then ride a perimeter circle of about a one-mile radius from the camera. I was searching for game trails and signs of presence.

In returning, I would review the chip to see what the camera trap had captured. The skunk certainly was an attractant. I had every imaginable wildlife species investigating the lure—from birds to bears and everything in between.

I monitored that camera for approximately two months, replacing the attractant with another road-killed skunk three times.

While monitoring the trails, I developed an understanding of how and where the predators were moving through this area. The test sight became a routinely traveled area for the predators as they seemed to be routinely monitoring the sight as well.

Although the breeze only picked up in the afternoons, its direction didn't seem to have any effect on the approach or exit from the area for the investigating wildlife, developing a conclusion that the lure's scent permeated in all directions rather than just being carried in the afternoon breeze, developing an added appreciation for the wildlife's olfactory system.

By establishing the lure, its known location, and my confidence that the wildlife had become accustomed to the attractant the table was set to begin the test.

The first thing I did was to ride in again at midday and remove the attractant. I brought some tools: a small rake as well as several thick garbage bags. I removed and packaged tightly all the evidence that I could find, except for the camera.

I left it alone for fourteen days and then returned to exchange the chip. Upon reviewing the chip, the wildlife, as well as the predators, kept returning and were captured on camera.

On the next camera check, I rode the perimeter as I normally did, checking the game trails and the presence of tracks. This time, I placed a deterrent throughout my circle. The deterrent was a fabric softener in its concentrated form.

The camera was left well into fall and routinely checked, and the scent that was used as a deterrent was freshened on each monitoring trip with a new scent.

Once I applied the scent, there was an occasional bird flying through but never again a picture of any type of predator.

The scent had worked as a deterrent, establishing another effective tool for discouraging a predator's presence and diminishing the predator livestock encounters.

Monitoring

I realized through the testing how valuable monitoring was and effectively applied it to my own personal use as well as applying it to some other ranchers that had been following my efforts.

It develops a routine of recognizing small but telling signs of presence. It also sheds light on the scope of the area that these predators travel and their interactions with other species.

So many of these signs are often overlooked simply because we are usually occupied with the daily activities of ranching.

Some of these signs, such as tracks, scat, avian presence, and even species of birds, roadkills, or the posture of neighboring cattle all may indicate presence.

One might think when we talk about tracks and scat that we are focused on the predators. Actually, I look at the cattle's tracks and their scat as much as looking for signs of predators.

The cattle's signs will tell you about their disposition and their direction of travel and speed of movement.

We often believe that predators want to be as far from human presence as possible, but in reality, humans present many opportunities for predators. Whether it's stray animals or pets, trash or roadkill, the predators adapt to the fact that humans equate to opportunity.

Desensitization

I don't believe that adapting to their environment is habituation. I believe habituation occurs not at the opportunity but rather when the predators become desensitized.

Desensitization happens when an action is repeated and the animal becomes aware that this action poses no threat to them. Through the desensitization process the action, whatever it is, removes movement and promotes a calm resolve. Actually, promoting by such actions is a comfortable and inviting place for the predators. Repetition is a key factor in desensitization.

I just had a cattlemen's meeting where a board member told me of a rancher that blasted an air horn every morning and evening to scare any wolves away. This action is an excellent example of an action that has a greater chance of promoting a draw rather than a deterrent.

Desensitization is a usable skill, such as in applying the stockmanship to enhance the *defensive posture of the herd group* and the *standing solution.*

By understanding of how not to promote desensitization in the placement of the deterrents will greatly increase the deterrent's effectiveness.

The key to not promoting desensitization when applying a deterrent is to keep the deterrent presenting an unknown. The unknown engages the *self-preservation instinct* that creates a reaction rather than an action.

Fear versus Abuse

I have been told by some that there is no place for *fear* in working with animals. In my more than fifty years of working with them, it tells me that's not possible.

Fear is an instinctual response for all living creatures, released from the *instinct of self-preservation*. It is why we don't step off tall buildings because it's a shortcut, or we get nervous when climbing on a ladder.

Anytime that instinct is summoned or called upon, the reaction is *fear*. That instinctual response can present itself at any time. Our effort is to instill a solution through developing a working relationship that presents a *calm and safe response*.

Whereas *abuse* is an action or an effort to punish or mistreat an animal through intentional behavior or actions—only promoting *fear* for no other reason other than trying to engage submission as a response, never establishing a trust or a working relationship with the animal.

Our objective is not abuse but rather to develop the desired response when the response of *fear* is engaged.

Through our training, the effort is to develop a reaction to *fear* that promotes a calm resolve.

By promoting pressure, we engage a response. Once we achieve the desired response, the key is the release of that pressure. This training tool is called *pressure and release*.

By releasing at the correct time, you set to memory the proper response.

By using the desensitization skill and a proper-timed release, we promote a calm *defensive posture of the herd group*.

Predators Evolution

Predators or carnivores have evolved by exploiting the *instinct of self-preservation.*

By manipulating that instinct and promoting *fear*, they then can engage the response of *flight or fight* to their benefit. By creating *fear*, it promotes an individualization that they can then exploit.

By presenting an unknown to the predators, we also can draw on an instinctual response from the wolf or any predator to engage *fear* and its responses. Both solutions draw on the predator's own instincts of *self-preservation. Scenting* as well as the *defensive posture of the herd group* are both intended to draw out a reaction rather than an action.

By understanding and managing the instinctual reactions of *fear*, we can present such solutions that play out on both sides of the predator livestock encounter.

Making Cattle Tougher

Among my first thoughts when beginning my research was the idea we needed to put horns back onto our cattle. Changing our selection of replacements that are destined to become working mothers and selecting a more aggressive individual.

I followed that idea of "straight on" confrontation for a while, and then I saw a video of wolves in Yellowstone taking down a mature buffalo bull.

Having worked with buffalo on one of the ranches that I managed in my younger years, I realized how defensive they can be. The video made a quick understanding for me that breeding tougher cattle wasn't the solution. A mature buffalo bull is far tougher than anything we could breed, and why would we want to?

That video of the wolves taking down a mature buffalo later helped me in understanding the wolves' requirement of engaging the individual and the *chase sequence.*

Bulls, whether buffalo or beef, individualize themselves routinely from the herd although I haven't witnessed many beef bulls that had been harassed or injured by predators.

Through the years, I have only seen one such attack. It was by a lion. The next week, that lion was killed at a federal facility in Livermore, California, as it was stalking people.

Although the bull that was attacked and was severely injured and required a vet's attention for several weeks, the lion was unsuccessful in obtaining such a substantial prey victim. A pack with multiple predators rather than an individual would certainly have been successful in securing the objective.

Lions also require an individual, but lions are more apt to use stealth and surprise as their tactics when securing their prey. The lion probably sneaked up on the bull and then engaged the bull by surprise.

I assume it's a challenge for predators to promote the chase, as the bull already has a natural *standing solution* in its disposition of being a bull. This may account for the lack of seeing many predator encounters engaging beef bulls.

Multiple Layers of Deterrent

By presenting layers of deterrents, you increase your odds of successfully mitigating losses to any predator. Each layer of deterrent strengthens the chance of engaging the *self-preservation instinct* of the predators.

As I had mentioned before, the objective of presenting a deterrent to the predator and it being successful is that the deterrent shall engage an instinctual response.

If one of the layers presented desensitizes rather than engages an instinctual response, it greatly reduces the other layer's effectiveness.

Diligence

Any presentation of a deterrent takes diligence in its placement and maintenance for it to be continually effective.

Whether applying occasional tune-ups to continue an effective response of *predator awareness* or presenting a new and unfamiliar scent, both can be maintained while monitoring. The effort must be a serious commitment.

The effort in placing or establishing any deterrent is an *all-ornothing* action. If the predators become aware of the opportunity, they will do what predators do and exploit that opportunity.

CHAPTER 4

Wolf Distribution and Microclimates

In my early research and at the beginning of the working circle, I met and talked with many local people that were from a multitude of different vocations. Many of them had concerns about the effects on Siskiyou's natural environment that the wolf may bring.

Many of these folks' jobs had them in the outdoors, and they would have sightings or see some *hearsay* evidence as to their presence.

They would let me know so my range riding efforts could adjust to address the predators.

Many that had concerns about the wolves' presence soon became interested in this concept of a community effort. Part of this effort was an information network that would assist in reporting sightings. In a relatively short time, I realized a pattern arose. That pattern had slight predictability on where the wolf would be in relation to temperature and season.

I was told that the wolf could endure subzero conditions but would shade up and rest during the heat of the day. The sightings that were being reported to me had the same similar daily temperatures. With the seasons, the sightings would have west to east movement using elevation to regulate temperature. On a daily basis, their movement would be north to south, remaining in a microclimate zone of consistent temperature. It appeared to be a subtle suggestion that climate and the season was a factor in the location of the wolves.

California compared to other states that have a wolf presence is quite different in its geography. California goes from sea level to Mt. Whitney, the highest peak in the lower 48 states, presenting twenty-four separate climate zones. But the zones that are relevant to Northern California and Southern Oregon and their ranges are the Mediterranean 0-2000', the Inter-Mountain 2000' to 3500', and the Alpine 3500' and above.

Because of California's geography and its two main geographical structures—the Sierra Nevada and the Coastal Range, and in Oregon, the Cascades, as well as their Coastal Mountains—the daily temperatures and climate zones move with elevation in a north to south direction. With these very expansive north-to-south temperature corridors, the wolf may travel great distances. Whereas the seasonal temperatures move in a west to east direction, providing the wolf's preferred temperature throughout the year. Achieving a comfortable and preferred temperature by simply traveling relatively short distances for such an able traveler. Although these seasonal corridors move west to east, it moves the wolf to a new country with the change of each season.

OR-7, being collared, attested to such seasonal travel patterns.

Much is stated about the wolf and its required prey of elk. California does have elk, but California also has many other opportunities for a species that capitalizes on opportunity. It may be that the wolf who can endure subzero temperatures when given the choice would prefer a more desirable habitat. Possibly people that may take vacations from the Northeastern States to such places as Hawaii or Florida through the winter months could understand such a concept. The suggestion is the microclimates afford a preferred temperature. It doesn't mean that the wolf is not capable of venturing outside of those parameters. It's simply a recognition of behavioral tendencies.

These microclimates have very predictable patterns. The seasons offer some predictability in the corresponding daily temperatures and their relation is to elevation and the season.

Understanding that the wolf prefers cooler temperatures, one could predict its absence in such places like the Sacramento Valley through the summer. But its presence there could be seen in December or January.

A Challenge Arose

This relationship between these microclimates presents another tool in the toolbox of mitigating risks. One of my leases for grazing is in Ashland, Oregon. It's well within the rogue pack's domain. The rogue pack encounters a couple of my grazing leases. This pack is known for preying on livestock.

The intended use was winter grazing at Ashland, but the wolf's presence there and the required weekly scenting just became difficult to manage. Traveling from the Klamath Basin to Ashland requires crossing the Cascade Range in the winter months. The summit crosses the Sierra Pacific Crest trail. Pulling a trailer loaded with horses certainly adds additional challenges to the trip. But too often, the passage was just not possible as the roads were simply closed, jeopardizing the routine of re-freshening the scent deterrents with an ever-changing scent, simply inviting desensitization and habituation.

Unintended Benefits of Range Improvements

The solution was to graze there when the pack was absent through the summer.

We had been working on a star thistle problem that came with this lease. Through the years, we had managed to reduce the infestation, but we were still addressing it each year. By moving the grazing to the dry season, the only available green grazing was the star thistle. Grazing the green adolescent star thistle was the cattle's first choice. In grazing it prior to bloom, we all but eradicated it within two seasons.

In the effort of mitigating risk from wolf presence, we enhanced the range's performance and effectively managed a botanical encroachment of an undesirable plant species.

A friend of mine and an extension adviser told me on several occasions that I had a unique ability to think outside of the box. My thoughts are that challenges are what feed our *quality of life*. Challenges are simply opportunities that afford the chance for solutions.

Perception

The livestock industry within California is quite unique when compared to other West Coast States and the Northwest. California's size as well as its various climate zones pretty much mean that somewhere within its borders, there is green grass growing every day of the year. That means that the livestock industry, which has been here since the Spanish control in the mid-1500s, has well-developed grazing areas available year-round.

This abundantly available resource lends itself to a more diverse industry than many other states, simply for the reason of the available grass while the others states have winter.

These same seasonal microclimates that have made California so desirable for so many for so long began with Spain's hide and tallow trade, cattle.

Many people don't realize that before the end consumer purchases that product or orders that steak at their favorite restaurant, many owners have had a part in bringing the consumer that final product. The national average is six to seven different owners.

Each owner is like a step on a ladder and takes their small piece toward the final cost of the product.

Many believe that the operation that begins the process, which is the cow calf producer, that those producers are the ones who are supplying the stores and restaurants with those products. This pasture to plate concept is relatively a new marketplace and basically is still in its infancy.

Consumer demand for accountability of where and how the product is raised and brought to the end consumer is building in popularity. But as the producers realize those added values, they're also forced to accept the added management issues that come with each step of climbing the vertical marketing ladder.

The financial reality of the marketing ladder is even though you may realize a higher gross return, you also incur added expenses as well as risks.

Traditionally, the cow calf producers operate with a yearly sale of their product, an annual income that comes from the sale of a healthy, weaned, and marketable calf. This product varies in size and quality but usually is around a six-hundred-pound calf.

Such an operation keeps and works with these mother cows on a continuous yearly schedule year after year. Depending on your market's demand, that demand is what determines the calving date. There are other reasons for calving dates, one of the states' most concerning issues is the *pajaroello tick* and *foothill abortion*. This pest may have more severe consequences than any predator. Its interactions with the stock result in *foothill abortion*.

The fall calving period provides a solution to this pest. Although recently, great headways have been made to develop a vaccine for this problem.

The many climate zones affect not only the marketing demands but where a predatory risk would be probable.

Many weaned calves will be purchased from other states and brought westward to California's abundant winter grasses. Those calves depending on where they were raised will vary in size from three hundred to seven hundred pounds.

These lighter-weight calves allow for a greater grazing density on this native feed simply because of their size. If a mature cow and her nursing calf require 3 acres for the season and we equate the mother and calves' total weight as 1,500 + 300 = 1,800 pounds. A 500-pound calf is 1,800 pounds divided by 500 is equals 3.6 calves per 3 acres.

If we had a pasture that would run approximately fifty pairs through the winter season, that pasture would be approximately 150 acres. As a stocker operation, that high-quality ground could support 180 hd. (head) of stocker calves.

Stockers should average on a good year, a 200-pound gain. That's a gain of 36,000 pounds versus the cow calf gain of 10,000 pounds. It's easy to see why the premium feeds go to stockers.

These stocker operations are usually in the lower foothill areas that run the length of California. Either on the Coast Range or along the westside of the Sierra Nevada. They usually are brought here in the fall and will be shipped out to other destinations in the spring.

The predators having the ability to comfortably move through these microclimate zones through the seasonally acceptable temperatures suggests that a probable confrontation is likely.

The cow calf herds are seldom run on these stocker quality pastures simply due to the economic issues and higher rents these stocker quality grounds bring. California's cow calf producers usually are in a bit of a tougher country. That tougher country provides the cow calf operation a very good setting at a lower overhead.

This perspective, although quick, is related to these microclimates and is intended to provide an insight into future concerns regarding these apex predators.

Another concern for many of these stocker operations is they are purchased calves.

Small bunches are bought from different producers and are often from different states. These calves are then put together as a uniformed lot. That uniformity, though, has nothing to do with a herd posture.

Through this process of obtaining these stockers, their individualization, as well as sorting, processing, and shipping, has been repeated routinely. Developing them to be a very desirable participant in the livestock versus predator equation.

CHAPTER 5

Predators

A Predator's Tactics

Each predatory species has its own preferred techniques for acquiring its prey. There is evidence that testifies to each species and its methods. The only common factor in the equation is that all the predators require an individual prey victim.

Investigating a Depredation

When a game official investigates depredation, they usually ask you to cover the carcass, limiting further damage by birds or other scavengers. The investigation is then as close to the actual facts of the actual depredation as one could investigate without actually seeing the take.

An investigation will begin with the initial observations of injuries and where those injuries are on the depredation. Although wildlife, as well as livestock, can be taken by predators, we will focus on the livestock. As most wildlife depredations aren't investigated or even found, often, in short order, those depredations are totally consumed and enter into the cycle of life quickly.

What we are investigating as far as the livestock is first, what is the size of the victim? A mature cow and an immature calf are different in the effort to secure each of them. The size of the carcass has relevance, to which predator has the ability to secure the more sizable animals. The mature animal, as an adult cow, is only able to be preyed upon by certain predators—either a lion, wolf, or bear. The coyote may scavenge a mature animal but cannot secure a healthy mature cow.

Along with identifying the injuries, the investigation shall take note of the surrounding area by the carcass. Depredation that is done by a mammal predator will most often be a violent event. The surrounding areas will show a lot of disturbance. There can also be pieces of the animal surrounding the area, as pieces are often torn off as the prey victim is trying to escape.

Without significant signs of disturbance around the carcass, the investigation lends itself to a greater possibility that the carcass may have died from natural causes and been scavenged rather than being depredation.

Scats themselves don't qualify the sight as depredation, only that the specific predatory species was at the scene. What happened is yet to be determined as a naturally occurring death or a death inflicted by a predator.

The national average for natural losses of livestock is 1 percent. So there are other possible reasons for finding a carcass, but that's the reason for an investigation.

When we find injuries, those injuries often lead to early identification of the predator. But not every carcass will present obvious signs of predation.

The site has many pieces of evidence. It's the investigator's effort to piece those clues together and come to a conclusion. Sometimes such investigations require forensic conclusions to qualify what occurred. Such work is done off-site and will require lab work that takes time.

There is also the possibility that the site has been visited by multiple species and shows no definitive conclusion as to which was the actual predator. Often, when bears enter as scavengers, they often disturb any conclusive evidence.

A Predator's Behavioral Characteristics

The obvious signs of a predator's behavioral characteristics will be in the following. These predatory characteristics are basic descriptions of each species' tendencies of securing their prey during predications. As with any event, the specific facts could be found to be considerably different. This is just a general summary of each predator's normal actions in securing prey.

It's always important to remember predators are opportunists. If any opportunity presents itself, any predator will not hesitate on seizing the moment.

The Lion

A lion's prey will have either puncture wounds on the carcass's back or neck from the lion's front paw claws. Sometimes those puncture wounds will be stretched out into long slashing cuts, leading to the rear of the carcass. Often, those cuts will be located on the sides and occasionally on the carcass's belly. The lion grabs the individual prey with both front paws, often one on each side. The lethal blow comes from a penetrating bite to the back of the neck.

A lion's attack usually covers a short distance and often starts from the advantage of surprise. Oftentimes, if the pursuit is engaged, it will be a short chase sequence and often downhill.

Often, a lion's depredation will be found on a westerly facing slope. The twilight hours help the predator in promoting the required stealth and achieving the surprise attack.

Depending on the size of the livestock, the lions will often drag smaller carcasses away from the kill sight and try to hide the carcass, either by covering the carcass or even hanging it in a tree. With a little backtracking ability, the sight will show the signs of engagement and takedown.

The Black Bear

A kill by a black bear will show bites on the back or neck. The bear's preferred method of securing a healthy individual is a chase sequence. The bear has an uncanny speed for its size. I personally have seen a large sow run down a calf with ease. My fastest horse would have had a hard time catching up to that calf. The entire run was about a hundred yards. The bear obtained the calf and never missed a stride as she disappeared carrying the calf over the ridge.

Finding a carcass from bear depredation is possible but not probable. The bear's social structure allows other bears to share in the feast, making short work of any evidence.

Bears are also significant scavengers. The signs around a carcass should show signs of struggle and violence, but oftentimes, the bears chase the prey over an extended distance, making the kill sight quite large.

The species of bears don't have a domestic counterpart. For that reason, their actions can't be compared with *behavioral tendencies from a domestic similarity.*

Canines

When we reach the wolves and coyotes, we get to the species of canines. Canines, as other predators, require an individual. I often hear comments about wolves killing multiple animals. They may, but that occurs one at a time, each time preying on an individual, certainly not killing all the prey victims in one fell swoop. The required individual is still key in this predator's successful depredation.

Working on ranches in the west, the word coyote is for *Canis latrans*, but the word also applies to human behavioral characteristics. It implies a thief, a sneak, or just an untrusting individual. The connection between the human characteristics and *Canis latrans* itself is the predator's ability to gain access and then exploit any opportunity.

There are many stories about wolves, and children's fairy tales are full of wolf stories. The elusive nature of the wolf only helps to promote and enhance the mystery. Such mystery only invites the imagination to perceive all types of boogeyman events.

The wolf is a capable and adaptable predator. But like all predators, it does what it does.

Canines as a species have *behavioral characteristics* that spread across that species. Within those *species characteristics*, domestic canines can lend some insight into those *behavioral tendencies*. Some of those challenges that domestic canines present have relevance.

The Chase

Every predatory species utilizes the *chase sequence*. The action puts the *predator* into a *nonconfrontational* position. From that position, the *predator* is in control. The intended prey is only responding to the instincts of *fear*.

The only *predator* that I am aware of that may seek the *fight* rather than *flight* may be the grizzly.

But I believe that the *defensive posture of the herd group* would effectively deter grizzlies as well. The *grizzly* is certainly a formable *predator*, but it has instincts just as any other living creature.

The instinct of *self-preservation* engages responses in all living creatures. The grizzly would be no different.

Canines have an unusual draw to the chase. When we look at the domestic dog that has a problematic behavior of chasing cars, it shines some light on the instinct of the chase and its importance to canines. This *chase sequence* is an instinctual response rather than a planned action, giving a little more understanding of the intensity of the *chase* event.

Often, when we find a dead cow, its dying posture may have relevance to the investigation. Realizing that the *chase sequence* is an important part of a predator's repertoire, the cow's positioning might suggest depredation even though there are no visible signs of injuries and the surrounding area is undisturbed.

The cow, if chased long enough, will use up all the oxygen throughout her body. This is called *hypoxia*. When this occurs, it is a life-ending event. We believe that a predator hunts for food, but this type of depredation may show no obvious wounds or consumption rather than only the cow's positioning.

Often, the cow will be lying on her sternum, and her front and hind legs stretch out in a position much like simulating Superman in flight.

We talked briefly about the speed at which the bear has. That speed quickly overcomes its victim. *Hypoxia* is the result of running too far and using all the oxygen stored within each cell of the body.

The bear's chase would be a short and a quick event, whereas the wolf would be a long-drawn-out chase, lending to the investigation that *hypoxia* is a depredation clue that points toward a sign of a wolf's *chase sequence*.

The investigator may skin the hind end of the carcass looking for muscle damage from bites, which is also a wolf's tactic of promoting the *chase sequence*. If the investigator finds no bite wounds or signs of violent death, they may come to the conclusion that this was not depredation but rather a naturally occurring death.

From my experience, this is depredation. Cows don't run their selves to death. This event would take an invasive act such as the *chase*. The problem then becomes, with no evidence what predator is responsible? I believe the probable answer would be an inconclusive finding.

As we realize that all predators utilize the *chase sequence*, some predators' efforts discount their ability for depredation by *hypoxia*.

The *lion's chase* is usually too short of a distance to cause *hypoxia*. The *bears*, having speed as well as brawn, probably would not need the distance. The chase, which creates the *hypoxia* itself, as well as the nonconsumption of the prey victim, points back to the domestic canine's problematic behavior of chasing cars.

Through the process of elimination and the *wolves'* ability to travel long distances, the depredation is not conclusive but certainly is probable that the wolf was the predator.

Often, an individual cow can easily be scared into this *chase* without inflicted pain or the cow may initiate the *chase sequence* by chasing the wolf to start with. Many cows will chase domestic dogs. Those cows set themselves up to become an easy prey victim for predators, especially the wolf.

Many believe that this *predatory* action is *killing for fun* because the predator did not consume the kill. I believe that the wolf functioned on instinct rather than fun, much like its domestic counterpart who chases cars. The action has nothing to do with hunger but rather a *canine behavioral characteristic* of being drawn into an *instinctual chase sequence*.

Barking

The *canine species* has another *behavioral characteristic* of barking. We are all familiar with a barking dog. Those of us who use stock dogs prefer the dog's work quietly as opposed to barking.

Barking happens to be a sign of insecurity in canines. When we're talking about the ranch's stock dogs, pups who bark as youngsters will often end up working quietly. With age, they acquire more confidence, and with that confidence, the barking goes away.

Through the years of training dogs, I will attest to the fact that a pup will often bark when the cows present a challenge. Often, for the young pup, that's when a cow faces him.

This *behavioral characteristic* of barking also sheds some light on managing an effective deterrent.

Instincts and Responses

Realizing that a facing cow brings forward insecurity for a stock dog pup during training is key in understanding the species' *behavioral tendency* and why wolves seldom pose frontal assaults on their prey victims.

If it's a *species characteristic*, that presents insecurity to the pup. It is a representation that such a posture from the prey will draw on the *instinct of self-preservation* for the wolf.

Along with the instinctual draw of the *chase*, the two propose a solution to *behavioral tendencies*.

In my experience, the only time that I have seen an assault on the head of a cow was from feral canines that resembled pit bulls.

Presenting a conclusion that canine predators prefer the *chase* and engaging or assaulting the hindquarters or the flank section from an attack position from the rear.

This from-behind-attack position is for the predator the least threatening in obtaining or securing the prey.

The question then becomes, How do we interrupt the instinctual *chase sequence?*

By engaging another instinctual response such as the most powerful instinct for all living creatures, the instinct of *self-preservation*.

A Solution

By establishing a response with the training of the *standing solution*, we summon the instinct of *self-preservation* within the predators. By the training of the *standing solution* and *seeking the herd group*, we establish a solution for the livestock that the herd group is a safe zone, giving the stock an escape position that promotes a calm resolve. The herd posture then transfers the *fear of the moment* away from the stock and returns it to the *predator*.

These defensive postures, as well as *scenting*, have proven to be an effective deterrent against all predators not just canines.

The Pack

For the wolf, there is also the fact that sometimes they hunt as a pack. The pack promotes competition among the individual predators. That competition also elevates an individual's confidence, emboldening the predator's actions.

A pack's *chase sequence* can secure and subdue the toughest wildlife as well as livestock when a pack is engaged on an individual. There are plenty of internet videos that attest to the severity of this capable predator.

For that reason, I believe the effort should present layers of deterrents rather than relying on just one to effectively discourage depredations—first by deterring presence by scenting and then by subverting an engagement.

Missing Stock

Many times, predators will leave no evidence of depredation. The count after gathering will just be short.

This short count is not uncommon for most ranchers who operate on large ranges, as this short count is a routine occurrence from year to year.

The common reason for the short count is just that the stock hasn't been located yet. The short count is followed by the search for strays, finding small bunches that eluded the gather for some reason or drifted out of the range's parameters.

The stock will often be with neighboring cattle or reported as strays.

For the ranching community, this is a normal event. It doesn't throw up any red flags or concerns until the missing stock is just never accounted for. Then the missing stock presents more of a question than a concern. I wonder what happened. Predators, theft, or are they still out there and we just haven't found them yet?

This unknown generates speculation, and speculation is guided by bias. A conclusion may not be the correct conclusion but rather only a statement of what the rancher dislikes the most. That list could include thieves, poachers, neighbors, and not predators. By not acknowledging a predatory problem, such a response concludes that there is no need for a solution.

Doing Nothing

This presents a scenario that will be to accept the losses on a continued basis, establishing and promoting the cows as easy prey and inviting a predator's presence. Such a set of cows can become the focus of a predator's interest.

If you're next to this operation and make the effort to train your cattle and present deterrents to deter presence, a predator such as a wolf may never enter into your parameters.

The fact is, it has all it requires with cows that are easily engaged.

A *behavioral characteristic* of animals is repetition. Repetition is sustained by comfort, being comfortable within the surroundings.

The cattle that supply sustenance and are an easy *prey victim*, along with no outside challenges, only promote a comfortable setting. This promotes a behavior without correction. That behavior becomes *habituation*.

Once you have reached *habituation*, often a deterring effort may be a moot point, as the predator's comfort level at that site has already been established. The effort of presenting an unknown to summon the *self-preservation instinct* may not be possible.

The predators certainly will not seek other livestock for the simple reason of seeking a more challenging opponent. That behavioral characteristic of seeking a more challenging opponent is only unique to human behavior.

Reactionary Responses and Desensitization, Curiosity, and Seeking Opportunity

Wildlife is reactionary. Those reactions are the response to the *instinct of self-preservation*. That instinct summons an instinctual response of *fear* that has the reaction of *fight or flight*. This instinctual response is why all wild animals are elusive. These instinctual responses are a response to the element of *fear*.

Predators may be considered more elusive simply because predators have a more sensitive awareness of their surroundings because they are predators. Their heightened awareness is a result of seeking opportunities and being aware of their surroundings.

If we present a deterrent that establishes itself as an actual *nonthreat*, the predator will become desensitized to that specific deterrent. *Desensitization removes* movement because the element of *fear* is gone. The repeated actions and nonthreat then become a comfortable place to remain. This is *desensitization*, which will progress into *habituation*.

An animal's *behavioral tendencies* will be the first to *react*. Repeating deterrents quickly miss the opportunity of engaging the predator on an instinctual level, and the repeating action becomes a recognizable nonthreat. That deterring device has quickly become a *desensitizing device*.

The predator not being threatened will stop and look out of *curiosity*. That *curiosity* is because the device is a novel experience and it's simply a new encounter.

This stop or nonmovement is the same as *pause and tensity*. The only difference is the removal of the *tensity*. Without the instinctual connection of *fear*, the only thing left is *curiosity*. That *curiosity* will require further investigation.

The apparatus actually being a *nonthreat* promotes comfort. The *predator* is then free to seek out *opportunities* within this comfort zone—promoting presence rather than deterring it.

Understanding Actions

By understanding *behavioral tendencies*, as well as a *species' behavioral characteristics*, we can begin to formulate effective deterrents. By engaging instinctual responses rather than just presenting a desensitization device, we address all predators with the unknown. By not subverting our own objectives of preventing losses, we present a firm stance against any predator achieving a successful outcome.

Predatory Behavior

The animal kingdom is governed by the moment. Whether the animal is domestic or wild, what guides their actions is due to instinctual responses or a stimulus to perceived pressures.

Behaviors are guided by instinct as well as a trained pattern of action. Such as the behavioral patterns that have been shown by their herd group or the pack that they were raised with.

By observing the actions of the pack or a herd group, those lessons become a behavioral pattern. Those same actions or responses not only apply to such things as hunting techniques but also apply to responses to deterrents.

Stimuli are what drive daily desires such as hunger. Such stimuli are the reason for the hunt or depending on the species, grazing or browsing, but any perceived pressure could result in movement.

Instinctual responses such as procreation or self-preservation, those responses are placed above pressures and stimuli within the animal kingdom.

Daily stimuli such as hunger are overpowered by these powerful instincts.

An example would be your thoughts of standing at the top of a building before lunch, looking over the side, and seeing a hot dog vendor twenty stories below. Realizing you're hungry, do you step off the building to get a hot dog, or does the instinct of self-preservation make you take the elevator?

The fear of death overpowers the stimulus of hunger or other pressures.

So even if an opportunity is presented, the response of fear would overpower such stimulus as long as the instinct of self-preservation was engaged.

The instinct of self-preservation brings forward the response of fear. Fears responses are fight or flight.

Fear itself is a response that's difficult to measure. Just as with humanity, what scares one may not scare another. The only component that generates an equal response is the fear of death.

Understanding fear is actually the first step in overcoming it. That statement in itself means for a deterrent to be effective, it must present an unknown, and that unknown must remain an unknown. By understanding what generates a response, one can then present it or address it. By attempting to understand it, we can also discover ways to use the knowledge to our benefit.

In presenting a deterrent, the unknown is the deterring factor. By not allowing an understanding, you draw forward an instinctual response of self-preservation.

By remaining an unknown, we engage the response to fear, which is fight or flight. Without actually presenting a life-or-death situation, only presenting an unresolvable threat.

Oftentimes, we humans relate a good deterrent to what we perceive would scare us, thinking that it should equally scare the animals.

Many times, what we present is an item that in all actuality is a desensitizing device. Mechanical repetition is one that's quickly understood. Much like the thrill of an amusement park ride, the first ride may be thrilling, but the repetition soon diminishes such thrill. By the act of desensitization, we actually promote a comfortable environment for the animal we're trying to deter. Once an item is recognized as a nonthreat, that item then promotes a secure area for the predator, establishing a comfort zone.

Trained Characteristics

We talked a little about trained behavior a bit in the above. There are certainly trained techniques to acquire a predator's prey. By witnessing these actions as subadults, the technique is shown and will be practiced until a successful outcome prevails.

There are also characteristics that are specific to each species. Felines could be said to have a stealthier style of tactics, intertwining surprise into their hunting practices, whereas canids apply a scareand-chase type of sequence.

The predator will follow the species' behavioral characteristics. Each predator must follow the species' behavioral tendencies, but several things span all predators.

1. Instincts—each predator has the instinct of self-preservation

2. Fear—although some perceive that predators have no fear, fear is actually an instinctual response, and predators do have instincts.

3. All predators require an individual to be their prey victim.

When we place or apply deterrents, those deterring efforts are most effective when we address each predatory species on an instinctual level. Drawing forth the instinct of self-preservation is a valuable tool in deterring presence.

Presenting an unresolvable unknown as a deterrent to deter presence, we also draw an instinctual response from the predators. Think of it as telling a story of the *boogeyman* to the predators in a language they comprehend.

Scenting is how to achieve an effective deterrent for presence.

Then by changing and developing our stockmanship skills, we can also develop a response to predatory pressures.

By eliminating the prey (our stock) from being individualized, we establish a deterrent. The *defensive posture of the herd group* challenges the act of seeking an individual victim.

The *herd group* itself challenges an individual predator. If the stock has been trained properly, multiple predator pressure should strengthen the *herd's* resolve and deny the predators the ability to successfully individualize our stock.

Predatory Imprinting on Livestock and Herd Dynamics

This study began a few years back as a discussion between a Ranching neighbor and myself. The question is how can a predator move through livestock and the livestock remains undisturbed yet a domestic dog will have the same set of cows quite unsettled. I have witnessed this livestock predator relationship through the years with every predator, except a mountain lion.

So in asking many professionals about this, there was no specific name to this interaction. With that said, for this discussion in this article, I am going to refer to this behavior as *predatory imprinting*.

The goal of this interaction is not a thought process but an instinctual behavior. But if we understand the mechanics of this behavior, we can apply such techniques to our advantage in handling our livestock as well as preventing this interaction.

The reason to avoid this interaction is that *predators* are opportunistic. They use this interaction to gain acceptance into the herd group and close presence with the livestock, building on and creating a window of opportunity.

If such an opportunity would arise, they would be in a position to capitalize on it. An opportunity that comes to mind is the cow being comfortable with such presence leaves her young calf unattended to graze. In which case, the predator has established its accepted presence and is then given the opportunity to capitalize on the opportunity presented to it. The effort doesn't require stealth in stocking but simply the absence of the mother's defense.

The predator by establishing itself with *predatory imprinting* has convinced the livestock that there is no reason for alarm or concern with its presence, removing the defensive posture of the herd.

There is a mechanical process that the predator applies to achieve this skill of *predatory imprinting*. With time and *indirect pressure*, the predators show a perception of nonaggressiveness and even an uncaring attitude toward the livestock.

Although the livestock may make an initial move toward the predators, creating a retreat in the predator's position. That retreat is simply a mechanical step in the process of desensitizing the stock. That retreat is stopped as soon as the cow's aggressive intentions stop. And a slow methodical approach or encroachment is begun again.

Then the predator often stands or moves in a slow parallel movement, recreating the *illusion* of an uninterested presence, thus establishing a firmer position of *predatory imprinting*.

By establishing a presence, it is a benefit to the predator's objective. Be assured that the predator's objectives have no desire for peaceful coexistence, only the opportunity to do what predators do.

The livestock is only a prey interest to a predator and the possibility of future opportunity.

Granted a coyote is not interested in a mature cow, but it is interested in her calf or the aftermath of birth. The coyote helps establish *predatory imprinting* for larger and more capable predators. It is not a coordinated effort of the predators, but it creates a developed response of the predator livestock's interaction. This interaction of predator and livestock only creates opportunity, which all favor the predator's position.

This interaction of *predator imprinting* has an effect on the herd dynamics. It could be suggested that this behavior skill is actually a loosening agent for the defensive posture of the herd group, initiating the first steps of individualization that is the first step in predation.

Observations of cattle that are in highly coyote populated areas show a very spread-out grazing pattern. The defensive posture of the herd group without intervention is lost until the apex predator reinstates fear and the chase sequence, rekindling the fear reaction among the livestock, which creates the response of a predator trained *standing solution*. This posture of predator awareness (when applied by the predators) is not a desirable event.

By understanding that *predatory imprinting* is not an innocent or an indifferent action we can start to address the action for what it is. The primary introduction by the predators that our livestock will receive should have already been established by us. Without our interaction and training, the predator's presence will be accepted and established.

By interrupting the *predatory imprinting*, we can help block this predator livestock interaction. This understanding that slow and indirect parallel pressure and occasional retreat will help us as stockmen achieve a trusted position. The predators themselves have shown us this study in settling and removing tension from our stock. As a stockmanship skill, we can learn several things by observing this predatory behavior. It is how the predator introduces themselves to the livestock that establishes the predator's presence. It is an indirect introduction with slow parallel movements and small retreats from a safe distance. Slowly encroaching into the livestock's flight zone with the perceived lack of interest for the objective. It is in fact the opposite pressure of a *chase sequence*. This action, if applied by the stockman, helps settle and promote a calm, accepting herd group, where the training of *predator awareness* may begin.

Through the years, the main solution to the problem of livestock predator interaction has always been directed at the predator. The predator now being protected by law only leaves the option of resolving the conflict from the livestock's side. Years of predator control have created these regulations that now protect these predators. Our stockmanship may be the last chance but may be the best solution.

If you think of this *imprinting* action as a conversation without words but rather with movement, then you realize that with any conversation, there is an introduction.

That introduction is the precursor for how the flow of the conversation will follow. If it begins aggressively, then the response will be fight or flight from our livestock—just as it would be for yourself if someone approached you in a threatening manner. But if it begins cordially, then the response can be the beginning of a new conversation or for the stockmen side where training may begin.

I have talked about this introduction before in *developing the herd*, an action or introduction to the livestock, such as settling cattle prior to an NCHA event.

The aggressive move would be the direct line of approaching the cattle. The *imprinting action* would be an indirect line of approach, *indirect pressure*. This approach may take some initial following or stopping (getting ahead of the cattle) if the cattle are sensitive. Sensitive or flighty cattle would be cattle who have movement upon the first sight of your presence. These cattle will need extra *imprinting* effort to accept your presence. But the same indirect movement outside their flight zone is how you establish *imprinting*.

This effort of *imprinting* is its own effort. If *imprinting* is the goal and the cattle are sensitive, make it the only effort that day. Don't think that while you're processing these cattle, we will imprint them too. Remind yourself about a conversation and the introduction. You would not expect to meet someone at the grocery store and drag them to your corrals to start processing cattle.

Remember, we are opening a dialogue of *imprinting* and preventing future depredations. This method needs to have the same priority as any other management event. Don't schedule other things in the same time frame.

Once you have completed several sessions of imprinting with your sensitive cattle, you can begin the introduction of your *predator awareness training assistant*. Calmer and more gentle cattle will be ready for the introduction much quicker. The next step will be *establishing the herd*.

It is my thought that predators instill fear and fear's reaction of fight or flight. The predators require our livestock to respond in an instinctual way. The predator requires an individual to prey upon. By training our livestock with a reaction of seeking the herd group when they receive a predator's presence or pressure, the livestock themselves avert a confrontation.

Much is said about *stress* in the livestock industry and its inherent losses to the predators. By training and instilling a response and a reaction of grouping into a defensive posture upon such pressure and stress, we interrupt the reaction of individual flight that the predator requires. The *defensive posture of the herd* then becomes an asylum of calmness and security, averting the stressful attempt of predation.

CHAPTER 6

Fear

Managing the Response of Fear

Often, I hear the comment that there is no place for *fear* in working with animals. I believe that all living creatures have instincts that govern their behavior.

Fear is the response to the instinct of *self-preservation*. If we're aware that all living creatures have instincts, the reasonable conclusion is that the response of *fear* is always a possibility.

It is my conclusion that the statement of "There is no place for *fear* in working with animals" is not possible, just as the *instinct of self-preservation* simply can't be removed or dismissed. Those instincts and their connection to the individual animal are part of the whole package.

Although I believe that in *working with animals* that there is no place for *abuse in using fear* as a tool in obtaining an animal's submission.

As long as the animal draws a breath, the instinct of *self-preservation* exists. Our awareness of not engaging in an instinctual response will keep the response of *fear* in check.

I believe that *low-stress stockmanship* begins here. By not challenging the instinct of *self-preservation*, the response of *fear* is never engaged.

Low-stress stockmanship is about how our actions affect the stock's responses. *Predator awareness* is about our actions affecting not only our stock but the interactions of our stock and the *predators*.

Fear is definitely not required in working with animals, but it doesn't mean it can't be summoned.

Do Predators Have Fear?

Many believe that predators are fearless. The fact is, all predators are elusive. That elusiveness tells me that they're not fearless, and their instinct of *self-preservation* may be even stronger than our domestic animals.

Often, time and maturity resolve many fearful situations. Those situations summon the *instinct of self-preservation* and can call up the response of *fear*. Those reactions seem to degrade with life's experiences.

For that reason, working a young set of steers or heifers will be different from working a set of experienced older cows.

That knowledge and experience of the domestic stock can also be equated to the predators. The behavior of an older individual can shape a subadult's actions, just as keeping some older cows with the steers or heifers during the first few workings, which can help settle the youngsters as they learn the routine.

This same training of the subadults by the use of an elder's experiences can be applied to deterrents.

Continually placing an effective deterrent will establish that *this area is off-limits*.

The elders will relay by their wariness to the subadults their concerns, effectively passing on the reactionary response to a given area or stimulus.

Pressure and Release as a Training Tool

Many times, in training animals, we use methods such as *desensitizing. For example,* when we apply this method to young horses, we use a tool such as a saddle blanket or flag. The mechanical repetition and the calmness we ourselves present with the release of such pressure (*stopping the flagging or sacking out*) promotes a calmness that we can use toward our goal of developing a working relationship.

The flag or the blanket is the stimulus, which is the pressure. Stopping the action is then the release of that pressure.

By applying pressure and then the release when the proper response has been found, we establish a connection of how to find relief to such pressures.

By presenting a calmness after presenting a stimulus and releasing such pressures as the flag or blanket and then reassuring the young colt "*You're all right,*" then by leaving enough adequate time for the colt to set to memory the proper response, we can successfully overcome the youngster's fear of such a stimulus.

Possibly the greatest win in this game of horsemanship is by presenting fear and assuring the youngster that he's all right. We then begin building a working relationship of trust.

Such trust is from the resolve of such a scary situation. Although we ourselves presented the scare to the colt, it only realizes that we both conquered that fear together.

Such a mechanical repetition presented as a predatory deterrent will suffer the fate of desensitizing the predator instead of deterring them. Making the area an understandable and comfortable place to be. In short, we present a doormat that says *Welcome.*

Our Approach

When we approach stock, that approach is like an introduction as if we were meeting an acquaintance on the street. Our approach is a pressure, just as we released that pressure to calm the colt by stopping the flagging and assuring the colt "*You're all right.*" A disengagement of pressure, like stopping or moving from side to side or even backtracking, relays to the stock the message of "*You're all right.*" The *direct line* and *aggressive* approach only initiate the beginnings of low-level *fear*, such as *pause and tensity*. That *low-level fear* is then the basis for building an escalation of an instinctual response from the stock.

Our goal should be as with our colt, as well as our stock, building and developing a working relationship of trust.

Developing the Proper Response

In the example of a colt's desensitization, we begin to understand how we can develop the *defensive posture of the herd group* for our stock. Rather than a flag or a blanket, we will use something to simulate a *predator's pressure*. We'll call that training aid a *pseudo-predator*. They are the *flag* or the stimulus. Their job is to mimic a predator, engaging the instinct of *self-preservation*. With the release in our control, we can develop a response that we are seeking which is the *standing solution*.

By establishing a preconditioned response, we set to memory a reaction to future encounters.

Any animals that we build a working relationship with, those relationships are from our presentations of the *solution* to such a stimulus or pressure. As with *pressure points*, which generate a *predictable response* with the particular pressure to each specific spot, our development of a *solution* to a predator's pressures will engage practiced conditioning, which is the *solution*.

We often hear the saying "*Understanding your fear is the first step in overcoming that fear.*"

The Goal

Our objective is not allowing losses to predators. This has two key components: overcoming the *fear* in our stock and developing a *solution* that will replace their fear.

By preconditioning the stock, we strengthen the faded instinctual response of seeking the *herd group*. That grouping of our stock presents a challenge to predators.

The second part is actually the initial effort of deterring a predatory presence in the first place.

We meet this challenge through the predator's olfactory system— placing an unfamiliar and man-made scent that is foreign and an unknown stimulus within the natural environment.

The goal is to challenge but not engage the predator. In that way, we present a questionable situation. The unknown summons a low-level *fear*, summoning an instinctual response.

This stimulus is a completely strange and new encounter, not in any way connected to the stock or ourselves. By changing to a different scent routinely, the predators will not become desensitized. By keeping the response purely instinctual, to put it simply, we create a bump in the night. That bump draws forward uncertainty and an unknown. That brings forward a *low-level fear*, which engages an *instinctual response of fight or flight*. As this unknown is presented and there is nothing to *fight*, it leaves only *flight* as a response.

If the predator achieves an understanding of any deterrent, it provides a level of comfort, *understanding your fear*, which encourages presence and future habituation.

Whether it's establishing a *defensive posture of the herd group* or deterring a predator's presence or even working on our horses or stock's handling ability, our understanding of *fear* is a useful tool for understanding the animal's perception of any given situation.

Allowing the Predators to Set the Preconditioning Pattern

Allowing time in between such training sessions sets to memory the animal's response. This time is called a dwell time. When called upon in future requests, it will have set and strengthened a preconditioned response or *solution* to such a stimulus or pressures.

This memory, if established by the predators before our training, can be used to the predator's advantage.

The cattle will set to memory a preconditioned response of *flight*, drawn from the instinct of *self-preservation*. This predatorily instilled response is then difficult to remove or overcome.

Any pressure will engage the instinct of *self-preservation*, engaging the response of *flight* or *fight*, making the cattle very spooky and difficult to handle.

With that predatory instilled response, our stock becomes an easy prey for the predators.

The problem with the predators setting the stock's initial response is that all our *stockmanship skills* relate back to a preset response of self-preservation, engaging *fear* constantly.

The Solution

By presenting a *solution* to such predatory pressures prior to the actual predators, we establish a calm resolve and a safe response for our stock.

Any situation that is new can summon the *instinct of self-preservation*. The response to this instinctual calling is then our preconditioned response of the *defensive posture of the herd group* and the *standing solution*.

By establishing a preconditioned response, we establish a *safe zone* that presents a *calm resolve* for our stock, reestablishing and engaging a natural posture for herd animals rather than leaving it to the predator's design tactics and promoting the response of *fear*, which successfully creates individualization with the actions of *fight* or *flight*.

Practice

We practice preconditioning in many ways, whether it's practicing working with low-stress stockmanship with our stock or practicing with our horses in the many horse-based events. The practice and time spent could be thought of as training.

Remember, *understanding your fear is the first step in overcoming that fear.* The preconditioning or practice establishes a response to such pressures—presenting a challenge to the predator instead of an opportunity.

Passing the Fear

If we manage *fear* properly, we can take that *fear* and remove it from our stock and replace it with the *solution* of the *herd group*, developing and rekindling a natural comfortable area for herd animals.

Presenting to the predators a challenge, that challenge then creates a questionable situation for the predator. The *standing solution* then raises the predator's concerns and summons *doubt*. *Doubt* is the beginning of *fear*.

The *herd group* is the deterrent and a secure safe location for our stock. That summoning of a predator's instinct is the deterrent in and of itself.

Many have said that the predators will just attack the herd. I believe the predators at their best effort, will search to challenge and individualize the weakest link.

It's important to realize that all predators require an individual. Whether it's from the promotion of *fear* and engaging the response of fight or flight or whether it's the element of surprise, either engagement for any predatory species is based on capturing the individual. We as ranchers still have to manage our stock in a way that doesn't present a weak link. Older or stressed stock must be kept away from predatory pressures.

Predators will capitalize on any opportunity.

Guiding Behavior

If one stops and thinks about humanity and the relationship of outside pressures, either social or economic, those influences have a lot to do with guiding our behavior. You then realize that there are many subtleties that guide our everyday lives.

Predator awareness is about developing outside pressures and stimuli that influence an animal's responses.

The animal kingdom is ruled by basic needs and instincts, which are about sustaining and preserving life.

If we make an effort to guide such instinctual responses, we can effectively manage behavioral tendencies. Those insertions guide the predator's behaviors rather than trying to confront the predators on an individual basis.

Our personal quality of life is then elevated as well as our stocks. With the lack of such predatory confrontation, our stock benefits as well as our bottom line.

These examples of the range of *fear* across species, whether wild or domestic, is simply to point out that *fear* is part of every living creature's existence.

We cannot reason and discuss solutions with the animals we work with, but we can address their reactions that are guided by instincts. By promoting a response for our stock, we present to the predators a challenge. As to the predators, the requirement of the individualizing of a prey victim is averted.

By scenting, we can present an unknown or a questionable stimulus that is new and unfamiliar within their natural world. Such strange and unfamiliar stimuli create pause. That pause then unleashes tensity.

Without the de-escalation of the tensity, that tensity quickly becomes *fear*.

We ourselves are then performing *proactive stewardship* and managing *fear* on both sides of the predator livestock confrontations.

The Word *Fear* Engages Emotion

I seem to get a lot of responses when I talk about fear and training animals. Not to argue the point, but how can fear be avoided? I will say that abuse has no place, but fear is a natural response.

Understanding the levels of fear is tough, but think of your own reactions to fear. There is that response to surprise, like someone jumping out from behind a door and saying *boo*! Then there is something that threatens your very existence. Your reactions are quite different because the levels of fear are different.

Realizing that fear is there and ready to unleash a response gives us an opportunity to present a solution. Fear's responses are fight or flight.

We have all seen a person whose focus is on their phone. That connection between the phone and that person is what I want in the connection between animals and myself. I want that animal to want to be with me and trust me.

I want to talk a little about horses to explain my point. We have all seen the person who starts a young horse by overdesensitizing it. They have shown the horse every stimulus they can think of and the horse will stand, but when they step on and try to make it move, its feet are stuck.

The natural progression is to try to make it move, kicking harder or spanking it, basically leaving fight as the horse's only response since flight has been removed. Realizing how to connect to the animal prior to creating the problem would save a lot of effort in correcting the mistake. The horse's responses are linked to instinctual behavior.

This removal of movement by overdesensitizing is an effective tool for our stock. It interrupts the individualization and the chase sequence that a predator must have in securing its prey.

By using pseudo-predators, we present fear and a solution that suits our needs. By releasing pressure upon the stock, reaching the *defensive posture of the herd group*, we instill a reaction that is set to memory, developing the *standing solution*.

Many people believe that repetition is how to train an animal. I'm not so sure of that. The training tool that I believe in is pressure and release. By presenting the pressure and then immediately releasing the pressure, you provide a trainable moment. Too much repetition leads to the animal seeking other answers to what you keep asking.

An example is the overuse of the round pen—putting long hours of loping in a circle and then putting the horse away. The pressure is the long hours in the pen, and the release is you turning the horse loose. Training the horse that getting away from the training session is its release. The release is the reward, which in effect you just rewarded a nonbeneficial response.

I said that I wanted to use horses as an example. So I have a young mustang that I acquired from the "adopt a horse" program. This youngster was quite fearful when we first picked him up. Upon arriving at the ranch, he went into a smaller pen than he was used to at the BLM lot. This was all so frightening to the young horse, and putting him in the smaller pen took away the response of flight, leaving only the response of fight.

In the first few days, he would charge, ears pinned back, trying to bite. He was a serious threat. But engaging the youngster with a rap on the nose when he assaulted me and then disengaging immediately, he soon became comfortable within his own space, beginning a partnership. Soon, when I would pressure him, he would move away. When I stopped the pressure and took a step backward, he would bend his neck toward me. That small effort of pressure and release was an easy and comfortable solution to his reaction of fear.

By presenting fear with applied pressure from our pseudo predators, cattle soon equate the herd group as the relief to such pressures. Then the *defensive posture of the herd group* becomes a sought-after safe zone.

Understanding fear and its responses gives us an opportunity to present and develop a solution to the problem. Transferring that response to fear, which all animals have, from our stock to the predators becomes an effective deterrent.

The Previously Fearful Mustang

CHAPTER 7

Stockmanship

Low-Stress Stockmanship

We hear quite a bit about low-stress handling skills. There are a lot of situations that seem to get lumped into this low-stress category. Establishing the skills of deterring predators will require a more in-depth understanding than simply handling stock in a low-stress manner.

What is stress? Stress has a very broad definition. But it could be said that stress is a physical or mental issue that causes a physical reaction. The reaction could be movement, unsettledness, nervousness, or anxiety. All could be said to hamper the calm productive well-being of the stock.

Most would say that fear would be categorized as stress. Then what about pressure? If an animal moves from pressure, how do you define what the animal moved from? Was it pressure or the reaction of some level of fear?

Certainly an animal that is worked more often such as a show steer or an old saddle horse would have less significant movement from pressure than that of a green or unhandled individual. That may suggest that exposure to previous pressures may have overcome some of their ties to fear. Possibly reacting to more measured degrees of pressure.

A famous horse trainer once said, "Make the right things easy and the wrong things difficult."[1] This is the basic essence of *pressure and release*. In confinement, the pressure and release are easily defined. If you create pressure, the release can be created by you and attributed to you. By practicing pressure and release, you set the parameters. The comfort level of the animals is understanding that movement here releases the pressure, establishing low-stress handling. Out in the open areas that are not confined, the challenge becomes once the pressure is applied. How do you establish a definition of release rather than just creating a reaction of fear and flight?

In reality, how do you eliminate encouraging a *chase sequence*? Promoting a response to predator's pressures. The needed confinement can be implemented by using *pseudo-predators* to confine the stock's movement. The ability to promote the stop is the first step of training *predator awareness*.

It has been effectively taught and practiced that being aware of the flight zone and applying pressure outside of this zone can successfully move stock and is considered low stress.

---

1   Ray Hunt.

Most of the time, the distances of the zone increase outside of confinement. The response of the stock is a comfort level to pressure. But our awareness of the flight zones may not engage a response of flight but may rather just be creating low-stress movement.

Without evoking fear and flight, it is understandable that the stock will never relate such pressure to a response from a predator, effectively moving stock in a low-stress manner but completely missing in developing a prepared response to predators.

Many skills of good stockmanship may present situations that actually promote the reinforcement of learned behavior that relates back to predator/prey relations of promoting the *chase sequence*. Chasing and driving cattle can promote a *chase sequence* response in the stock and instill a reaction into memory that will be drawn on in a stressful situation, completely missing the mark of deterring predatory pressures.

Many times, slowing down is equated to low-stress stockmanship. By observing predators' interactions with stock, you soon realize that this is a predatory skill practiced by predators. I call this interaction *predatory imprinting* and *desensitization*. In developing a reaction to predatory pressures, one needs to realize the requirement of creating a response that is a reaction to the presence and not just pressure.

The training requires that the stock have a different response from the reactions to fear and the response of fight or flight.

By effectively presenting pressure to simulate a predator's actions, and releasing the pressure when they have achieved the defensive posture. This, for lack of better terms, could be thought of as practicing depredations. Setting to memory a response to a predator's pressure and presence. This is called *the standing solution*. While training another posture develops, it is a grazing reaction that develops a tighter grazing pattern. This is called *herd awareness*. Then finally, the *defensive posture of the herd group*, this is *predator awareness*. All these accomplishments can be trained with pseudo-predators. Dogs that work in place of the predators. Simulating a predator's pressures to create the defensive posture of the herd group.

This training accomplishes a response to predators. We engage in this act rather than the predator because we can provide a release, whereas the predators would only provide a far worse outcome.

If one's country can be successfully monitored by range riders, then that may be an effective choice. The principles of being an effective deterrent fall into the same parameters as *predator awareness training*. Human interactions establish a human presence that relates to the predators as scent—also establishing a herd group which itself is a deterrent against predators and monitoring on a routine basis.

The deterrent of range riders is one of the most costly choices, but many NGOs offer cost-share.

The requirements of a range that can support the range riders is its capabilities to water the stock and the ability to keep one large herd group together. The resource of stock water dictates how the stock can use the range. In much of Northern California and Southern Oregon, the stock water dictates that the stock water is in rotation or at smaller supply sources often many miles from one another. Often, forestry permits were designed this way to promote better range use, spreading cattle out evenly.

The range with limited water resources requires a different method of deterring predators. Such as scenting, the actual placement of a product that suggests human presence and a reaction by the stock of seeking the *defensive posture of the herd group*. The *herd group's* size can be as low as three cows. It's the *standing solution* that is important, not the size of the herd.

Fear is a component in every breathing animal. The predator is no different. The instinct of *self-preservation* rules. Presenting a situation that's new and unusual will evoke that instinct, telling the predator to move on.

The training of *predator awareness* is an effort to instill a response in the stock rather than relying on a reaction of the natural instinct of fear, which is *fight or flight*, relying on the calmness of the *defensive posture of the herd group*.

Developing a Herd Posture
(and Removing Movement)

Movement is intentional, whether it is grazing calmly or flight. Each action of movement has a reason for its occurrence. Stimulants are the reason for movement, hunger, weather, or pressure from encroachment into the flight zone or *perceived pressure.* They are all factors that create movement. We must have an understanding of what creates movement to manage it.

Removing fear is our objective and promoting the instinctive reaction of the *defensive posture of the herd group.* This is accomplished by desensitizing and replacing fear with a *standing solution.*

Creating the herd reaction of *predator awareness* first begins with developing a stance where the training can begin. This method of desensitizing is the same action as the NCHA (National Cutting Horse Association) uses in settling cattle prior to each cutting class. I call this action *predatory imprinting*

Or if you are a rancher who works your cattle horseback and your cattle aren't exposed to people on the ground that new exposure will create fear, this same method can help you prepare and expose them.

Areas that can be a concern are cattle leaving the ranch destine for sale yards, feedlots, or anyplace that they may handle cattle afoot. The fear will seem as if you have wild cattle and wild cattle no matter the quality are less desirable. You can use this simple method to calm and expose your cattle to humans working afoot, presenting a calmer and more valuable product.

Developing a herd or settling cattle, gentling or leaving them overnight or accustoming cattle to dog presence is all the same effort to removing the reaction of *nervous movement* from *perceived pressure.* It is about using steady movement outside of the livestock's flight zone (desensitizing). We talk a little about this a bit before.

This technique is *predatory imprinting.* Developing the herd is the first step so that we may begin the training of *predator awareness.*

One of the most common mistakes that defeat the effort of developing the herd stance is the direct approach, going straight to the livestock or running to get ahead of them. These efforts create a flight. Flight is what we are trying to replace with the defensive posture and the *standing solution* of *predator awareness.*

The training practice of desensitizing is a long-held practice of training behavior. But as with anything, done poorly, it can result in no results. Let's look at the practice of sacking out a young horse. The objective is to get the horse used to things moving around and contacting him. But done incorrectly, it is just a practice of mild abuse. Without an understanding of the desired results, there are no forward accomplishments.

In training one of the most common mistakes is overdoing a training session. We as humans enjoy results, so we continue the action to enjoy our achievement. The animal only understands that the repeated effort must require a different response. It does not instill a learned behavior, but rather, it relates to a bad experience.

With the horse being sacked out for the first time realize that when the horse accepts the blanket, stop. Give a moment for the horse to understand "this is it" before continuing.

When we are working with animals that may be in the beginning stages of a training level of *kindergarten*, we often ask for a *PhD* result. Understand that training is a progression of efforts over time. Another training practice is the practice of *pressure and release.*

The pressure is applied to achieve a reaction. When the correct response happens, the pressure is released. The release is the reward. Instilling that the correct response is set to memory. The release must come quickly, with an adequate time for the animal to realize "this is it" before continuing. This is called *dwell time.*

Whether you are calming cattle destine for a sale or creating the stance outside, it is the same method. If it's settling or calming cattle destine for the sale, you can start in a larger pen of your corrals. Get off your horse and at the far side of the corral, walk back and forth, crossing the corrals at a normal pace in a lateral pattern that applies no pressure to the stock. If movement is created *stop* and *stand*, when the movement stops, walk away and begin the lateral pattern again.

After several passes, move the cattle to an alley. The alley should be closed at both ends. Stand at the end of the alley and slowly proceed along one side. When you create the reverse parallel pressure, they will pass by you following the lead animal, often at a high rate of speed. *Stop and stand* when they have passed and are standing at the end of the alley with *no movement*. Proceed to the other end of the alley you were first destined for. Turn and slowly approach the cattle again, keeping to the side of the alley, recreating the *reverse parallel pressure*. As the cattle are passing by *stop and stand*, if movement stops when you stop, continue and proceed to the end of the alley. This will need to be repeated several times, but it will effectively expose cattle to being worked calmly afoot.

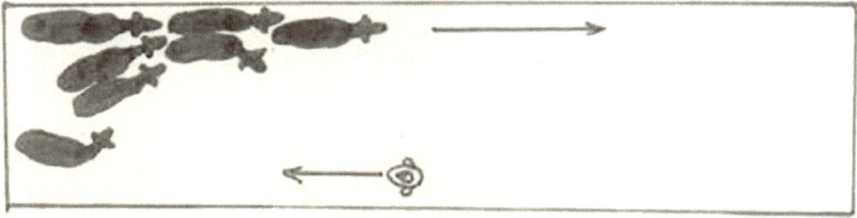

Alley work-reverse parallel pressure

When we are accomplishing the goal of herd development outside on the range, we don't have the luxury of a backdrop, such as a corral or an arena or any type of containment. Because the training is happening in large areas, it may cover a considerable distance, but we are performing this training horseback, not on foot. The training in open areas takes an understanding of the cattle's response and recognizing the edge of the flight zone.

The cattle will relay to you where that distance is. Depending on the cattle's disposition and sensitivity, which will tell you what the appropriate distance will be.

The cattle's first reaction is a recognition of your presence, which is usually an *eye-to-eye* contact, *stop and stand*, depending on the cattle's sensitivity. It is the determining factor in proceeding or backing up. If the cattle move with eye contact, then they are sensitive. Back up. If they remain standing or return to grazing, proceed from side to side, passing laterally to the outside edges of the furthest edge animals before turning.

This movement is the only movement intended for you the trainer. It should be started at a walk, and after the stance is sound with *no movement*, your efforts can be escalated to a trot, but never a run.

If this movement creates movement, you must stop and increase the distance of your separation between you and the cattle and begin again. The sensitive cattle will need to be approached again (stop, back up, and stand) until the response is just curiosity and a stance. Then proceed with lateral movement. If movement is created, back off again and repeat.

Once the lateral movement creates no movement, you may proceed by closing the distance at a diagonal approach. (This is *the gather*, bringing the cattle together) Your pace, as you get closer to the animals being grouped, should slow and occasionally stop and start randomly. When the cattle are grouped and standing loosely, the effort has been accomplished.

This is a very good time to quit. The appropriate number of *herd development trainings (where cattle stand calmly)* prior to beginning *predator awareness* training is three.

By developing a herd group, movement becomes an easy effort moving a herd group versus keeping individuals grouped together.

If your cows are not accustomed to dogs, this same *herd development* may be used to accustom the cows to them. The control of your dog is of great importance. No yelling or loud calling should be required. When a dog is not in the working mode, its proper position should be behind the horse ready and willing to respond to a command.

The introduction that you are arranging between the cows and the dog needs to be performed without disturbance. No other projects should be on the agenda, and no other guests present.

We humans can multitask and are comfortable with chatting while we work, but it is distracting to the animals whether it is the cows or the dogs. Both their attention should be focused on the introduction.

Once the herd posture is complete, cows are grouped, calm, and standing. This is the construction phase of *predator awareness*. You are building a foundation that further training can be built upon. In the beginning, moving forward too quickly will create cracks in that foundation.

Allowing several trainings of just establishing a herd posture will benefit the results of the *predator awareness* training in the future. We have established the *herd group*, and our next step will be creating movement. With the group standing quietly, it requires pressure to start the stock. By rocking your horse, short turns from left to right (it is preferred that the horse's front feet are the only movement), will usually start the movement. If not, walking in a zigzag pattern works well also. This is rear pressure point pressure. This action with further training will be discouraged. Pressure point pressure is a controlled response, but its actions are rear pressure and movement, closely mimicking a chase sequence. With further training, creating movement will begin at the lead and create movement with the *reverse parallel pressure*.

After creating movement and following for a short distance of at least two hundred yards. We will create a stop. By using forward parallel pressure outside of the flight zone (the *passing zone*), you will create a stop. This is most effective when done at an extended trot (*do not run*). If you are accompanied by a dog, send him at this time and allow him to proceed to the lead. After the cattle have stopped, remove all pressure. Allow the cattle to stand. You have just effectively created the *herd posture* and begun movement, and you have successfully accomplished the first training session on *predator awareness* and the *basic stop*.

You are on your way to instilling the defensive posture of your herd.

Pressure and Release

We hear a lot about pressure and release, in stockmanship or horsemanship. But it's often just stated but not really explained. The statement is a rather broad statement. The human's presence whether you're engaging cattle or horses is a predatory position. Depending on preconceived perceptions of the animal, how we react when we introduce ourselves dictates their reaction. In other words, if the animals have been trained to have a nonbeneficial response, we must back up and start over from the beginning.

One of the human challenges is understanding that our lives operate on a time line, places to be, and things to do. Animals, on the other hand, don't. Their goal in life is basic: eat, breed, and stay alive, self-preservation.

In order for humans to connect to animal interactions, we need to understand the goals. If it's a young horse that we hope to ride and enjoy for many years as a companion or as a working partner. We must realize that it is a long-term goal, not a short-term outcome.

If you think of the outcome as graduating from college as an individual who is ready for worldly interactions and the individual is currently in kindergarten, there is a lot of learning between the two stages.

Kindergarteners don't do trigonometry. The challenges that we present must be very simple. We must understand that too much challenge can't be absorbed in one interaction.

When we interact in the beginning, we must read and understand small achievements. Stopping and "releasing pressure" means quitting at that time.

If it's cattle that we are working with and trying to settle them and they are nervous from previous relations, realize that you must overextend the releases.

The release is leaving the animal free of our presence or pressures.

It also requires a dwell time to achieve an understanding of what happened. A day or two is a good dwell time for young horses.

With maturity, we can understand that dwell time shortens.

We must keep a consistent interaction of building a connection, just as playing with blocks, stacking one session on top of another, and building a sound foundation that will lead to a good working relationship.

It's important to understand that crowding and pushing the animal only promotes a nonworking relationship, promoting that "do as I say relationship" rather than working with partnership.

An example is cattle that won't go in the corral or threw a gate. Stop. Step back releasing the pressure. Hold for a time and begin walking back and forth slowly increasing the pressure. The pause in the movement is not simply resistance. It is a concern about a perceived stimulus or threat.

When you see a response, such as heads-up, stop again, allowing the cattle to settle and begin the release again. The repeated attempts and releases will help settle the cattle.

The release and the quit may be as important of a training tool as much as whatever the session's goals are. There is a lot of use of repetition with a lot of training sessions.

An example might be a horse's lead. Let's say we achieve the left lead with a young horse. Repeat it, then stop, allowing the young horse to understand the accomplishment.

If we keep working and repeating the action, the youngster will start trying other things, not understanding what you, the trainer, are asking for. The additions and repetitions can be added on in future sessions. It's better to quit early on good responses than to overdue.

Each future attempt will come to pass easier and quicker.

Pause and Tensity

Often, when we are working our livestock or horses, we often have a predetermined project in mind. Those projects have goals as well as a preconceived schedule of completion. We, as humans, operate with timely dedication. It has been something that begins early in life. "Be on time." Everything we have done throughout life is measured by time.

Our efforts at work become stressful if our planned allotted time surpasses its planned schedule, such as having to work overtime or having to work on a scheduled day off.

Our stock knows no such importance of time. Their perception is based on previous engagements and their perception of the moment at hand.

We as humans are challenged routinely to abide by the clock, whereas within the animal kingdom, there are no such demands.

The Problem

The problem is, we, as humans, often are so tuned to the challenge at hand, that we forget the stock we are working with and have no such understanding of the rush or needed effort to accomplish those tasks.

What happens oftentimes is the same thing as we talked about before with that individual who has to work overtime. That added effort creates stress. The only difference for our stock is that we relay that stress to our stock at the beginning of our efforts rather than at the end of the workday, making an elevated stress workplace for our stock throughout the day, further challenging our allotted time schedule, which leads to further pressure to accomplish our task, proving to create a challenging and more stressful workplace as the day goes on.

Understanding Pace

Whether it's cattle or horses, they have a daily level of comfort, which their movements and pace, as well as disposition, are derived. The efforts of movement are quite different whether they are relaxed in a grazing mode or whether they are being chased by a predator and running out of fear.

Both of those scenarios present different stress levels, but they also both affect the speed of movement.

The Challenge

The challenge then becomes meeting our goals of the allotted time and accomplishing the task at hand while not engaging in a stressful environment for the animals.

We often believe, that "when something is tough, the tough get going" or "what's required here is a bigger hammer" or simply "cowboying up."

All those solutions challenge the stress levels of the livestock that we are dealing with and only promote added conflict and pressure to an escalation of a stressful environment. Such a stressful environment promotes handling difficulties, which slow things down, compounding the problem in an escalation of stress for the stock.

By understanding whether our time allotments are adequate enough to accomplish the task at hand in a calm and effective manner is key to creating a low-stress event.

Whether it's gathering a large range or simply gathering a small trap, both are quite different as to the time that will be required to accomplish each equal task of gathering.

For example, I have often seen throughout the years in large ranges and tough countries when it's time to begin gathering. Often, the solution to such a challenge is to seek and ask more people for help. Going straight to the solution of "what's required here is a bigger hammer."

When, in actuality, what's needed is more time to effectively gather and clear portions of the range, so each day is about clearing a specific area and then gathering the next section on the following day, mimicking a multiday parade, progressively marching day by day to its conclusion.

Whether it's gathering or processing or shipping, the allotted time should be set as an effort to reflect the natural *pace* of the stock, allowing enough time to complete the task with ease, not challenging the effort to have everything go *just right* to see a successful outcome.

An Animal's Behavioral Tendencies

Oftentimes, we overlook an animal's behavioral tendencies because we are just too engaged in our own thoughts and challenges of the daily needs to put much thought into what's going on with the animals. We recognize obvious signs, as to health or stress or the effects of predatory pressures, but we often aren't aware of the subtle signs like the *pause* and *tensity*.

Movement is intentional, but stopping also has a reason for occurring. Our stock can relay their reason for their stop if we will take a moment to realize their body language.

Predator awareness is about instilling a response of seeking *the defensive posture of the herd group.* When this training task is achieved, it's more than just a set of cattle grouped together. The posture is a defensive stance rather than simply a group of cattle.

Movement has been removed, and the cattle's posture and positioning should be focused on the herd group, aware of their surroundings and the *pseudo-predators.*

The telltale sign of achieving this defensive posture is a *divergent stance,* each individual facing in a slightly different direction. When pressure from a predator is applied, the stock's response is the *standing solution.*

Whereas a group of curious cattle that are focused on something unusual in their daily encounters will also be grouped, the group's positioning will be all directed at the subject or that curiosity. This grouping, although a herd group, is no more a defensive stance than an untrained individual. Whatever the curiosity that is focused on, a simple fright or surprise would send individualized flight in every direction. This herd posture is not a prepared defensive stance.

Cattle seek other cattle for comfort. We can encourage the cattle to seek the *herd group* for safety. But the *defensive posture of the herd group* requires pressure and training with an effective release to instill a defensive response and posture, effectively instilling the standing solution.

Cattle can stop for many reasons, but another reason is *pause and tensity*. This action is a behavioral characteristic that could be considered a low-level fear. This *pause and tensity* affects all animals, not just our stock.

The *pause* is a result of an impending questionable perception. Something that raises the animal's senses to alert status. That heightened alert status creates a stop, a *pause*. Once the feet have locked up, the *tensity* begins. Any continued pressure will result in an *instinctual response to fear*, which will have the response of *fight or flight*.

An example would be pushing our stock through a gate or into the corrals. The group stops. That is the *pause*, but we push harder, elevating the pressure. Using that tactic of "what's needed here is a bigger hammer." Then the stock break out as flight is the response to the elevated pressure and stress.

This is also a young horse's common *behavioral characteristic*. The *pause* locks the feet while the *tensity* is engaged. The youngster's response will also be *fight or flight*. Managing this locked-feet scenario happens to be a fine line between establishing a trust or allowing an additional escalation of fear. Often, youth will choose just "cowboy up" as a solution, but with age, one might seek alternative solutions. I had made an example of the cattle approaching the corrals.

It was just intended as an example. The cause for the *pause* may be anything. It's about the animal's perception, not ours.

Our handling of this *pause* must be to *back off the pressure*. For cattle, a stop of the *rear pressure*, which we are applying must end, mimicking the stocks pause. Our movement should then be presented in a parallel or lateral presentation until the stock becomes settled and begin moving again.

As to our young horse when this pause happens, often, the young horse will seek your guidance. The personal challenge is the recognition of the request for help and your response. Horses have a much quicker response and reaction to a perceived fear than our stock. This instant as a trainer will develop trust or make trust difficult within the working relationship between horse and rider.

Possibly, at this time, many would try kicking or bumping the young horse forward, straight into the young horse's concerns. I believe a better solution would be to freeze the forward pressure, tip the youngster's nose, ask for a side step and be ready for the engagement of flight, and slowly curve back into the encounter again, developing a trust that you're aware of the youngster's concerns, building a trusted working bond between horse and rider.

Often, when we're riding a young horse down the trail or in a new environment, we as riders will become comfortable and complacent because our youngster is doing so well. The young horse also becomes comfortable, mimicking the content curiosity of the grouped cattle, all contently staring at an unusual curiosity. This relaxed pace invites a boogeyman event in the youngster's mind. The response is rather an instant reaction rather than a response to a perception of a perceived threat.

A possible solution to prevent this youngster's mind from straying to an imagined threat and a boogeyman event is to keep the youngster's young mind engaged in small tasks, such as responses to subtle pressures and releases, practicing the communications between horse and rider, giving our youngster's mind activity and preventing boredom and avoiding the boogeyman event.

This same behavioral characteristic of *pause and tensity* relates to *predators* and *deterrents* as well. The challenge in that scenario of being an effective deterrent is not allowing an understanding of the engagement of the stimulus that created the *pause*.

Presenting an unknown will create the *pause*. Preventing an understanding of the stimulus will add to the *tensity*, effectively presenting an uncomfortable situation for the *predators*.

As with our stock and horses, we may never be sure of what creates the perceived *pause* and *tensity* event. But for the *predators* and the effort of placing a deterrent, we become the creators for the reason of the *pause and tensity.*

The lack of understanding and the inability to resolve this perceived threat engages an *instinctual response of fear*, which has the response of *fight or flight.*

This *fear* draws on the *instinct of self-preservation*. From that initial perception, it doesn't allow the *predator* to become comfortable and proceed forward, effectively detouring the *predator's* route and its presence.

This behavioral characteristic of *pause and tensity* is subtle but understandable. Being aware of its linked relationship to the *escalation of perceived fear* makes it a useful tool to add to our skills in placing deterrents, as well as improving our understanding of an animal's behavioral characteristics and our applied stockmanship skills.

Whether it's the predators we are deterring or our own domestic stock we are working with, understanding the *pause and tensity* will aid us in accomplishing our efforts.

Pressure Point Pressure

When you apply pressure in reference to stockmanship, there are different responses. The direction of your applied movement as well as the *specific pressure point* that your movement is directed at. These both will determine the response. *Pressure points* are *not* about physical contact but rather your movement and position in relation to the stock. Your presence is the *pressure* that generates a response that creates a reaction of movement from the stock.

Will each reaction respond consistently? The answer is no. The response will be a reaction to the *perceived pressure*. The perception is from the animal who is receiving the pressure. The animal's perception weighs heavily on whether there is fear or the speed at which the pressure is presented. Many who work on stockmanship skills believe that *slowing down* is low-stress stockmanship.

Many Believe Slow Is Better

Slowing down doesn't always promote calmness or equal lowstress stockmanship. I believe, as with stock dogs that present their position or pressure with a lot of eye contact, the stock's perception is that they're being stalked. Untrained stock will move away from such pressure, and in actuality, it's the first step in promoting the *chase sequence from predatory pressures.*

Stock that has already encountered a *predator's pressures* will have been exposed to *fear* and will respond with *fear's* reaction of *flight or fight* and often try to fight the *stock dogs.* Moving forward through this established preconditioning from predators takes more effort, but a quick-moving dog will help settle down the unsettled stock rather than a dog that moves stealthier.

This same perceived stalking pressure can also be connected to other things such as the stockman themselves or ATVs or a horse and rider. The perceived perception from the stock's perspective is slow *perceived pressure,* such as a lot of eye contact and slow movement. A simple change of direction, going the other way, is needed to help settle the stock. We often don't realize we present predatory pressures ourselves, but something as simple as a dark pair of sunglasses may present an illusion of predatory eye contact with the stock.

Applying the skill of Predatory Imprinting

Calming the Stock

Predatory imprinting and desensitization are defined as slow indirect movement outside of the flight zone, leading to the desensitization of the herd. This is one of the predator's skills to infiltrate the herd posture. This is the interaction that accounts for predators being seen walking through groups of cattle. This *desensitizing action* is a response to *indirect pressure* in which the stock accept the predators, and the predators are allowed within the stock's instinctual flight zone. Understanding this predatory skill allows us as *stockmen* to use it to settle spooky cattle or develop a herd in the open.

The predators achieve the results of the skill *predatory desensitization* by using *indirect pressure*. *Indirect pressure* is the practice of appearing not to be interested in the stock, such as a coyote hunting for voles or squirrels as his attention seems to be other than the stock. The practice is a random movement with occasional direction changes and stops, slowly settling the stock to become accustomed to the coyote's presence. In a short time, they're encroaching well within the stocks flight zone.

The coyotes are, as all predators, simply opportunists, seeking opportunities rather than specific plans. Predators being allowed within the herd posture to inspect it for possible opportunity is not what I prefer. It's not at all unusual for stock that are not dog broke or accustomed to being worked with *stock dogs* to chase dogs but allow coyotes to walk through them unchallenged.

Using Desensitization and Pressure to Your Advantage

If applied prior to working on any *pressure point* pressure, this desensitizing skill will help calm the stock's *perceived pressure* and make the stock's response more consistent. The action of *desensitizing* is also the method used to create the *standing solution*. *Desensitizing* removes movement. Although in the case of *predator awareness*, we also encourage seeking the *defensive posture of the herd group*.

Granted that *slowing down* is often a good practice, but there are times such as working within a confined set of corrals. That movement must be kept at a quick pace to accomplish the tasks at hand.

Understanding your actions of presenting pressure in relation to specific *pressure points* and the desired reactions is the objective. Whether it's *developing the herd or creating movement* or training the response of the *standing solution* or simply benefiting daily management practices, whatever the stockmanship intention, an understanding of these *pressure points* makes the task at hand, less challenging.

Another point is rear pressure. Movement that is created from pushing. I will just say to that point. Isn't that just promoting the *chase sequence?*

I understand the question, then how do I move my stock? By developing a herd group and then creating movement and then simply following. By developing a herd posture, you develop and promote a group that moves as one.

How often have you seen rear pressure applied and fail? An example would be trying to get reluctant cows through a gate or into the corrals. The common response is to push harder and yell louder. This will often result in the cattle not moving or trying to escape in the opposite direction they are being pushed. Loud rear pressure actually draws the stock's attention toward the rear, inviting the stock to break.

Often, this interaction of *calling* to the cattle is the same skill used when separating the cow from her calf in the corrals, as in the task of *sorting*. In *sorting*, the gateman works a horseback in an open gate, only allowing mother cows to pass while blocking the calves. Done properly, the accomplishment has the cows sorted from the calves in a stress-free manner.

The gateman is working at the lead of the herd, only leaving calves back by blocking their exit and allowing the mother cows to pass.

The pressure for the reluctant cows is presented in the same manner as asking the cows to sort up. Training cattle to *sort up* is a low-stress skill that if done correctly saves time. The solution of trying to create movement by using harder and louder rear pressure is just directing the cows to come out as they have already been trained to do. This breaking away with rear pressure is an unintended training event that the cows will repeat, again and again, promoting a spoiled set of cows.

These rear pressure positions, with all the best intentions, promote the predator's interactions with their prey, promoting a response of the rear pressure engaging flight, which predators will use to their advantage.

So as to the reluctant cows, I would settle the cows with lateral movement at the rear. Send someone into the lead and apply a pinch point separation of a dozen or so cows to develop a lead and create movement, then turn and apply the reverse parallel pressure to get the others to follow.

Lateral movement to settle stock

Cattle that are too sensitive, *spooky*, or cattle that are heavy, and *gentle*, both set up in favor of a predator's pressure, which has the intent of individualization and the *chase sequence*.

By using *predatory desensitization*, you can settle *spooky* cattle, and if the cattle are too *gentle*, *pseudo-predators* will help develop the *defensive posture of the herd group*. Both have been described in detail previously.

Flight Zones

The flight zone of stock varies from their breed and previous stockmanship skills that have been applied. The shape and distance of the flight zone also vary in relation to speed and direction and the strength of the pressure being applied.

An example might be a content-bred cow standing in a pasture. Her flight zone would be a 360-degree circle. When you approach, you would generate movement away from your position.

This would be the simplest of the flight zone explanations.

A simple flight zone

As you progress in understanding a flight zone, you'll soon realize that the flight zone reshapes itself, depending on the speed and direction of the pressure as well as the stock's perception. Adding *fear* into the encounter engages instinctual reactions rather than *pressure point* responses.

Mapping out an animal's pressure points is an effort to understand applied pressure and its reaction to a relative movement that the pressure will engage. Although the response is also about the direction, speed, and distance to the stock's flight zone. Each of those affect the end result, as well as the stock's perception of such pressures.

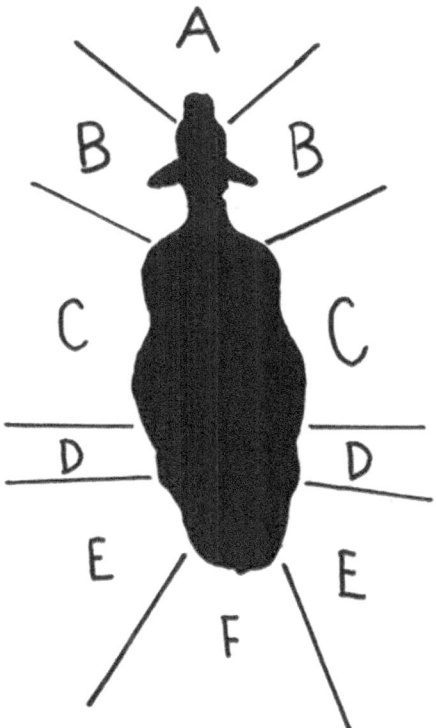

A)   This area of the face or the lead is the area from the stock's eyes forward. When the directed pressure is applied here when you're outside or in open spaces, the response is a stop of forward movement. In the corrals, its response will also stop forward movement, but it can make cattle back up when no other direction is an option.

Often, unintended perceptions of the stock will hinder the stock's forward movement. Many times, we are not aware of what's making the stock uncomfortable as we are processing or working with the stock. We only know it's difficult for us as well as the stock. That perception is a *perceived pressure* to this eye-forward *pressure point*, and it stops the movement. Engagement may be someone ahead in the processing area moving, talking loudly, or it can also be simply a shadow or something, blowing in the breeze or a dangling rope or pull chain. A solution may be changing your approach to your pressure, possibly simply loading the chute from the left side rather than the right. Simply redirecting the stock's attention to new and more effective pressure.

This is also the area our pseudo-predators will go to when stopping flight.

1. *The Stop*

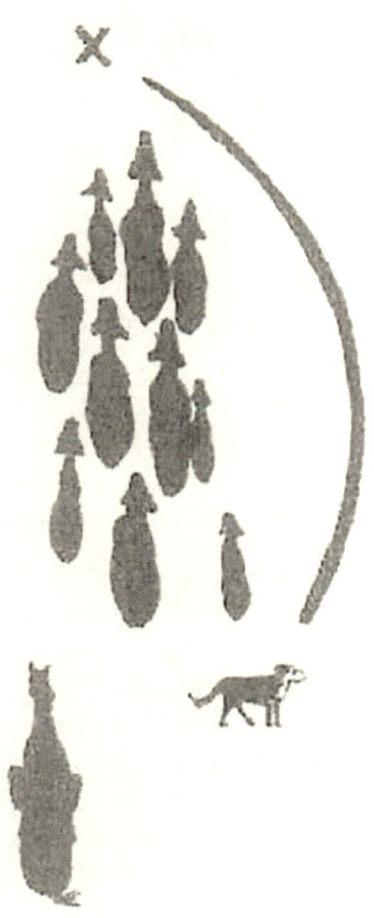

B)   This point is from the stock's eyes and runs to the point of the shoulder. It is the *pressure point* that has a directional response. Most often, when applying pressure here, if you are approaching from A, you will create forward motion in the opposite direction of your applied pressure. If you're approaching from C, you will begin a slowing of forward movement. Both are affected by speed and distance from the flight zone.

This area of B is a prime spot to generate movement. In an alleyway or crowding area, pressure here will engage movement. When using the skill of the reverse parallel, this is the area where the pressure leads to movement, and proceeding to the rear creates a follow from the rest of the herd.

Diagram 3

Reverse Parallel Pressure

Reverse parallel pressure creates movement in the opposite direction the pressure is applied. The speed created is the proximity to the flight zone. The closer to the flight zone, the quicker the pace; the further out, the slower the pace.

3. *Reverse Parallel Pressure*

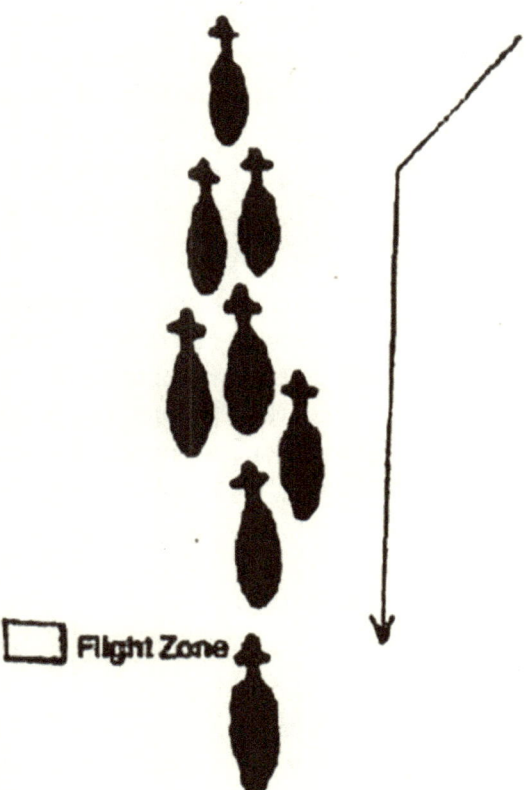

Flight Zone

C)   This side or ribs is the area that is the strongest area affected by your direction. Think of this area as a giant question mark for the stock. It is an area where the stock is measuring your applied pressure. If you are going forward from D, the stock will gauge your forward speed and closeness to their flight zone and begin to slow.

Outside of the perimeter of this *flight zone* is the *passing area*. Your direction becomes of no concern to the stock's movement.

If your direction is from B, your closeness will dictate the response of speed. The closer you are to the stock will generate quicker pace.

This rib area also affects lateral movement when an angle pressure is applied. This area will turn or create a shift in direction upon a *direct perceived pressure*.

D)   This is the flank area, possibly the most sensitive area. This area engages forward movement and elevates the perceived pressure of fear, engaging fear's instinctual reactions rather than a reaction to a pressure point pressure.

E)   It's the hip area, probably the most used pressure point. Its movement is forward.

F)   This area is a panic area. The response to fear is fight or flight. When pressure is applied with fear, it promotes flight. Elevate the level of fear and the animal turns to fight.

The previous map of *pressure points* (A) through (F) is based on an individual animal, but the herd group has the same *pressure points* when you have developed an effective herd posture. These *pressure points* will have a response much like moving the individual stock, but you'll be moving the herd as one giant individual.

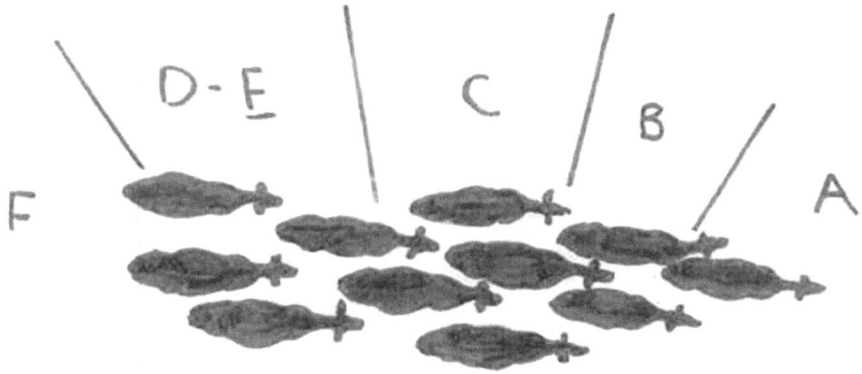

The *pressure point* of (F) functions better as a follower rather than a *pressure point movement* in respect to the herd posture.

Reading the Stock

Reading the stock is also an important part of achieving proactive results. Settling the stock prior to working them is a good hedge against undesirable responses.

Nervous postures and actions from the stock may present signals to the stockman that the stock are not ready to work calmly. Rather than *cowboying up and getting western*, a better response would be creating a herd posture. The objective of *predator awareness* is to instill the *defensive posture of the herd group* and interrupting the *chase sequence* and the *individualization* that the predators require.

Some postures may be ears forward or an elevated head, urinating or excretions, or simply walking or trotting away from the herd. These actions of individualization lend themselves to benefit the predators rather than promote the safety of the stock.

Nervous postures to the *pseudo-predators* is also a sign that the stock require more settling to canine presence. If the stock are unaccustomed to the use of *stock dogs*, then *stock dogs* will be the required initial effort. A basic concept of being calm with *dog presence*, that will be required to achieve the *standing solution*, in which the *pseudo-predators* can then instill the response of the *standing solution*.

Conclusion

By understanding our actions of applied *pressure point pressures*, we can help our stock have a more effective defense against a *predator's presence* and possible *predatory pressures*. The effort to better our handling skills will not only help in everyday chores but help mitigate the *predatory risks* that our stock may encounter.

The herd group doesn't always equal a defensive posture

I've been getting some responses about cattle already having an instinctual herd response, so there is no need for any further training.

Just a point about cattle being a herd animal and every grouping being the same as another. Possibly without a reference to why the cattle are in a group, one might assume that all groupings are the same and serve our purpose of a defensive posture.

Cattle are herd animals, and they use that herd posture for a variety of circumstances. Cattle will group because of weather, such as wind and rain or temperatures. They will also group to insect pressure or even curiosity. For herd animals, the herd group serves a multitude of purposes.

But one may assume that each circumstance is the same, but they're not.

When we are seeking the herd group for a defensive posture, it is quite a different structure and purpose than a set of cattle staring at a curiosity.

I am going to make a point about purpose and execution. I don't support or oppose anything to do with the comparison. It's just to show some contrast between preparedness and being comfortable but unprepared.

A response to fear

Let's say that a person might be concerned for their safety. The list of circumstances for such reasoning could be vast but understandable.

A possible solution to this fear may be a conceal carry. So one purchases a weapon. At that moment, one might find solace in their decision, but in fact, without additional training, that weapon is just additional weight to be packed around. This person without additional training really isn't any safer with the weapon than without it. Even if the person feels safer, the actuality is they're not.

The simple comparison is to the weapon in relation to the *herd group*, they both promote a level of perceived comfort, but without a basic understanding of purpose and function, neither the weapon nor the *herd group* serves a purpose. But with training, both can deter a conflict.

The true defensive value of packing a weapon is in the ability to be able to use it effectively if the occasion should present itself.

Without practice, you have no knowledge of defense, as the weapon itself will not defend you.

As to the simple engagement of any herd posture being a defense, any elevated pressure, *such as predatory pressures*, will only *engage fear's* responses, promoting individualization and engaging the *chase sequence*, promoting a successful outcome for the predators.

Just as one must practice proficiency with a weapon for defense, one must also practice a response for *predatory pressures* and instill the *standing solution*. So when the encounter happens, a trained response will be a comfortable reaction rather than an engaging response to *fear*.

By using a *pseudo-predator*, we can mimic a predator's interactions with the stock and have a controlling handle on this practiced event. Still invoking *fear's responses* but not risking a loss or any damage to our stock.

Preconditioning the stock, imprinting a response in case of such an encounter. By us controlling this practice session, we can effectively release the pressure when we achieve the desired response, creating a trainable moment.

Training or practice instills a reaction when such pressures present themselves, whether it's proficiency with a firearm or our stock responses to *predatory pressures*. The importance of a practice session is invaluable. But as with a firearm, improper use or unsafe practice can be detrimental to one's safety. We need to realize that when improper *predator awareness training* occurs, it can be a practice in inefficiency and promote a situation that benefits the predators.

The engaged responses should be followed by an effective and quick release. Before reengaging, we must allow a dwell time for the effort to be effective. Without those key components, the posture will not become a defensive stance but rather just a precursor to an elevated *fear*.

Just as one would not expect to become proficient with a firearm in one session or become an advanced marksman within a few. We as trainers seeking an effective response to a predator's pressures must go into the effort, understanding that training an effective response takes time and multiple sessions.

The controlled environment puts us in charge rather than leaving our stock to the efforts of a predator's pressures, preparing our stock in case of such an encounter.

By comparison, instilling a response into our stock isn't much different from obtaining a concealed carry permit and learning to effectively use that weapon.

Antiquated solutions

We have discussed *pressure and release* as a training tool. Such unintended applications of this training method are just as effective at establishing a comfortable area to remain, as they are too being a deterrent.

The problem with the misapplication of this training method is that it usually has consequences that counteract the original intention.

I have mentioned that repeating mechanical deterrents simply act as desensitizing devices, but actions can also achieve the same results.

An example would be an act such as intimidating or harassing a predator with no actual consequences. Without an actual penalty or consequence, that pressure is just a curious event, invoking curiosity rather than *fear*.

We may put 100 percent effort into the chase, but without some type of consequence for the predator, it is a nonthreatening event. Possibly just establishing a connection with a playful partner. We may believe that we frightened the predator, but actually other than our fatigue and momentary satisfaction, we simply performed an act of *desensitization*.

Such repeated action only becomes a game of chase, much like children playing "tag" or a domestic dog returning a thrown ball, like fetch. The action actually becomes comforting to the predators.

The interactions build a bond, so to speak. Much like coyotes learning the distance of a rifle shot. The event without consequences is simply a desensitizing event, establishing awareness and promoting a level of comfort from the understanding of the action rather than *fear* of the unknown.

When you think of a *canid* being comfortable with our actions, you actually don't have to look far, domestic canines often interpret our actions. The old saying of *being man's best friend* is because of their observation abilities. That trait is another *behavioral characteristic* of the *canine* species.

Encounters with the predators

Encounters with the predators are counterproductive. It establishes an understanding of our limitations and promotes comfort in being able to achieve their elusiveness without a lot of effort.

The achievement of the encounter is then relaying to the predators our inability to pose a serious threat to their existence.

The importance of the unknown

Our brief presence or contact with predators only benefits the predators. It provides an understanding of our vulnerabilities. Whether we are chasing or yelling or attempting to scare the predators, our actual effort is promoting ourselves as the weaker ones in the effort.

Our objective should be to remain an unresolvable mystery to the predators.

The *unknown* is our strongest ally in deterring presence.

The *unknown* engages an instinctual response rather than an applied effort.

Many will think that I'm speaking of keeping humanity as the unknown but not so. Humanity is well understood by most predators. Our personal scents, presence, or actions are all too familiar to most predators. In fact, I'm sure they see us, meaning humanity much more than we see them.

When I speak of remaining the *unknown*, it's referring to our deterrents, their placements, and applications.

We want our deterrents to present an unresolvable question. In this way, we summon insecurity. That insecurity draws forward an issue of safety for their welfare, which summons the *instinct of self-preservation*. With the engagement of the animals on an *instinct level*, thought and curiosity is not available. The *instinct* simply invokes a response.

Thinking about what we present

If we take a bit to think about our idea of placing a successful deterrent, we need to think about the presentation to the animal and its response rather than something that would give humans a fright. Humans enjoy frightening moments. It's a *behavioral characteristic* of humanity.

One doesn't have to think very hard for some of these examples: fairy tales, children's stories, haunted houses, amusement park rides, scary movies, and the list goes on.

Within the animal kingdom, a frightful event is a result of the response to the instinct of *self-preservation*. An actual fear for one's life. Anything less is simply a curiosity—very similar to humans slowing down at an accident.

Without the *fear* of death or serious injuries, the event becomes a curiosity.

Realizing that many of the canids species are governed by scent, we can use that knowledge to our benefit. Even though we humans can't quite understand its parameters, our knowledge tells us this would work.

Our sensory perception and the olfactory system are very small in comparison to the canine species, but even our diminished senses are capable of sensing extreme scents. We as humans manufacture products that are intended to be diluted when the products are used. In their concentrated form, they're so strong we can smell them through their packaging.

These *man-made manufactured* scents are completely strange and unfamiliar within the natural world. Because of their concentration and their ability to disguise unpleasant odors from us humans, their strength presents a frightening unknown within the natural world.

This engagement of a predator reaches an instinctual level rather than a curiosity or playful challenge that only invites a continuing presence.

Consequences and rewards

I will ask a question about safety belts. How many of you get into your vehicle and buckle up or put your child into a child seat before running an errand to town? That action, although not obvious, has been a trained response by society. The fear of injury or financial punishment, if caught by an officer of the law, has developed a response of buckling up.

The *consequences* are legal, fiscal, or the *fear* of injuries or worse. The *rewards* are your health and comfort of thought and lower costs, such as insurance premiums. Both are part of the same equation, the installation of a trained response.

Although we don't think of putting on our seat belt as a trained response, the fact is, that's what it is. We don't think about the action. We simply subconsciously do it. If something distracts us, the autodinger will remind us to buckle up. It has been a societal effort of training.

So I still hear from time to time about how you can't use *fear* in instilling a response or a reaction to a *predator's pressures.*

Just as society trained you to buckle up. When did someone come to you with strong-arm tactics and you simply buckled up out of *fear?* I would say that the *consequences* of not buckling up did more to influence your response to clicking than any abuse.

That same training method of *consequences and rewards* is the same as the training technique of *pressure and release.*

Training in the animal kingdom is about your actions, which have a response. Whether it's teaching a dog to sit or cows with the *standing solution*, neither requires abuse. You as the trainer are asking for a response. When it is achieved, you release, instilling a response to similar future encounters.

By simulating an encounter, you then have the ability to promote a successful response—an instilled reaction to pressure from outside pressures such as a predator's presence. By presenting pressure and then releasing when the defensive posture is achieved, you interrupt the predator-prey relation. Training a response to pressure, you intercept the predator's intention of engaging the reactions of *fear* with *fight or flight* and offer the stock a safe less stressful option of the *standing solution* and the *defensive posture of the herd group.*

CHAPTER 8

Dogmanship

Our reason for our use of dogs in the efforts of *predator awareness* is instilling a behavioral response for our livestock. That is when the stock encounters a predator or a predator's pressures, they will have a response. That trained response that we will have instilled shall become the stock's instinctual response of seeking the *defensive posture of the herd group*.

These dogs are quite different in purpose from our stock dogs and shall be called pseudo-predators. Under the trainer's guidance and handling, they will pressure the stock, and when the stock achieves the desired response, we the trainers will call for the release of such pressures. In a few sessions, the stock will respond to the *pseudo-predators* with this defensive posture simply on sight.

With further training, the dogs will strengthen the herd posture by seeking and shedding out individuals. This searching for a weak link provides an example for the *herd group* that being individualized is not good. This is key to the development of the *standing solution*.

Developing a response of seeking the *herd group* for safety and comfort.

This training activity is the same method of *desensitization* as when I talked about "sacking out" the young colt or a deterrent *desensitizing* a predator through repeated mechanical repetition. The action of quick movement and repetition of circling the stock or some may say baying the stock is *desensitization* of the stock. This *desensitization* creates the *standing solution*.

Desensitization removes movement.

The *standing solution* stops the individualization of the stock and interrupts a predator's engagement of the required *chase sequence*. It also challenges the predators because the response of the divergent stance of the cattle challenges the predator's *self-preservation* instinct. This is the job and the reason for the *pseudo-predators*, not engaging *fear* but rather providing an alternative solution to flight.

The *standing solution* and the calm resolve of the *defensive posture of the herd group* promote a solution to the predator's pressures.

What's the Difference?

A stock dog's actions are an extension of the stockman. By the stockman's direction, the stock dog assists in aiding the stockman in managing the stock's movement. Whereas the pseudo-predators stop all the stock and promote the *defensive posture of the herd group*.

Often, stock dogs will exercise their practice with a calm and stealthy quality, simply pressuring the stock with a subtle slow stalking movement. This pressure is pressure point movement even though that movement is in the direction that was simply asked for by the stockman. This action is assisting in the movement of the stock and is simply a *flight* in the preferred direction. In order not to elevate the stress level of the stock, the stock dog's desired actions promote calmness in the stock.

Our *pseudo-predators* are, in actuality, the complete opposite. The *pseudo-predators* are not stealthy in their actions. Their preferred actions seem in comparison to the well-trained stock dogs, to be fast and reckless, simply circling the stock at a much greater speed than the stock dogs. Their fast movement and pressures, as well as their stopping abilities, have the stock nervous and seeking relief from the pressures.

This action continues until a herd posture resembles a *defensive stance*. At that time, we, the trainer, must call for the release of the pressure. The *pseudo-predators* must have a good trainer's control, and the stop must be a quick and complete release when the trainer calls for it. This quick release and leaving enough dwell time sets to memory the correct response.

If one already uses dogs, that's good. If not and your stock aren't dog broke, I would suggest accustoming your stock to a dog's presence before the beginning of training. You could use *predatory imprinting* to accomplish this. See stockmanship.

If you're beginning to use *pseudo-predators* and you already have been using stock dogs, don't use the two together. Their actions being quite different actually are the opposite in intentions, which promotes confusion rather than training any response.

The Shed and the Block

The shed is an advanced *dogmanship* skill and something that most pups will simply not do.

The main characteristics of a pup should be speed and the heading action, the stop.

For pups or a dog that just doesn't get the shed, you, the trainer, can assist by searching for a weak link and separating it from the herd group. Your dog's response should be a heading action, turning the cow back toward you. Your action will be to block the return to the *herd group*. You and the dog shall accomplish the task of the added pressure to the individualized stock until the stock reaches the herd group for relief.

Effectively training the stock that anything outside of the *defensive posture of the herd group* is not a good place.

Diagram 4

The Block

By encouraging shedding and blocking, the return you are establishing that by being individualized the cow receives pressure. The reason for the block is to establish the understanding and encourage the desire to return to the herd. The return when aloud is the relief of pressure, establishing the herd as a safe and calm place.

4. Shedding

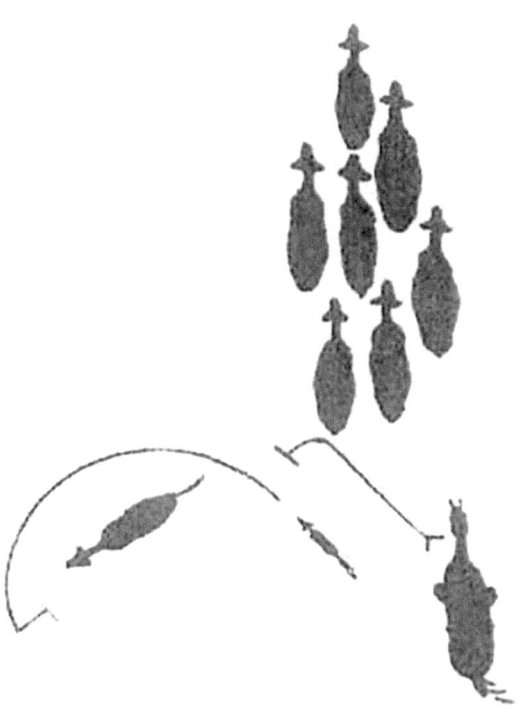

Training a Young Pup

If you're beginning with a young pup and you want a good effort, you must realize that everything a pup learns is a *show-me session*. So as you're beginning the first steps, that will be the stop.

So you, the trainer, must develop the *herd posture, create movement,* and then have the pup assist you on the *stop.*

1. *The Stop*

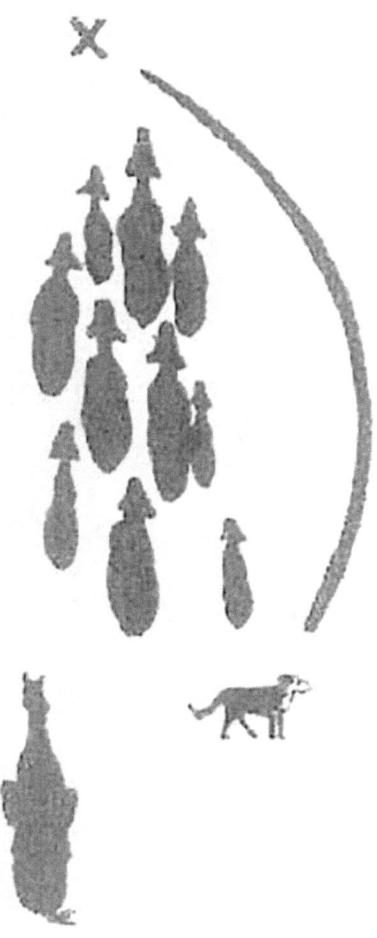

Within several attempts, the pup should understand that "we are going to the front of the herd."

A "listen up" should be in place from early on. Use the listen up to develop into a stop or hold for the dog and later a directional change.

The "listen up" is done as young of an age as possible, removing the pup from other pups or parents, when exploring is within its development stage. Individualize the pup and let it explore, with no interactions from yourself, then give a "listen up" command. I prefer a single-tone soft whistle as a "listen up."

The response should be a tip of the head or a slight acknowledgment of hearing the whistle. That's it. The acknowledgment reward that will be applied is simply nice stroking as you pick the pup up and return it to its littermates.

As you progress the reward for a 'listen up' will be just something simple, as acknowledging the dog with name recognition and one praise word, I like 'good'. "Sam, good."

I personally don't engage the dogs in conversation. I like to keep all our verbal interactions short and responsive. Don't overpraise or over-reward for the desired completion of a task. Simply say "Sam, good."

The same goes for admonishing. Leave the word no to only the most serious discouragements. I like admonishing with a tone rather than words. My preferred reprimand is *aughh*. The reprimand is quick and then not expounded upon. The break in action should be immediately stopping the dog's action. If I am on horseback and have no response, I will pull my rope and throw it as a baseball-only holding the tail, letting all the coils fly. That action usually doesn't require repeating, but it is the consequence of not adhering to *aughh*.

A Cellular Connection

I spoke in a previous chapter about my desired connection between the animals and myself. It's like that connection of that person who is focused at all times on their phone. That human behavior is the same attention that I am seeking from the animals.

Their attention must be to the task at hand, but my interruption to their effort must be recognized instantly.

This desired connection demands that I myself allow mistakes to happen, not seeking perfection but rather effort, then rewarding the effort rather than grading it. "Sam, good."

Often, I work with others who focus on obedience rather than performance. That effort in my mind loses sight of the objective. The pseudo-predator's purpose is to develop a response within our stock's reactions to a predator's presence.

That repeated command of "get behind" weakens the action of simulating a predator and the effort of searching the group for a weakness.

Our understanding is that the *pseudo-predator's* job is specific to the task of developing the *defensive posture of the herd group* and not being a stock dog is key to developing a successful solution to deterring predators.

To the Skeptics

When I begin a conversation about predators, my experiences usually give me a read on the person that I am having the conversation with and their reactions to my solutions.

Many times, they have already come to a conclusion, and no matter what I say, their opinion is set.

Then there are those who take a much broader stance, such as "Right, wolves kill cows, and there's nothing that you can do that will change that."

This second person is one who might understand my efforts if I put them into a more easily explained comparison.

I realize the second person's position and actually agree with them to a certain extent.

Let's go to cars—automobiles. Let's say we both have a nice vehicle. In many cases that car has become as much a part of the American dream as a home.

Many take great pride in the prestige that comes with their vehicle and understandably so.

Now in this imperfect world, there are many who would like to possess such a symbol of pride but can't come by it honestly. Those would be the thieves. They're looking for any opportunity to achieve such a possession. Understanding that thieves exist, one might try to protect their vehicle. One might even say that we are mitigating such risks.

We both have parked our vehicles on the same block. Although I have installed an alarm system in my vehicle and locked my car as a deterrent to the thieves, you, on the other hand, leave the windows down. The door's unlocked, and the key's in the ignition.

I believe that I have mitigated my risk to the best of my abilities, but as to your car, I would venture a guess that your risk is much greater of being stolen than mine.

Thieves are just that—thieves. Predators are just that—predators.

Simply presenting the opportunity and ignoring the risks seems to me to just invite such losses.

Mitigating one's risk changes nothing other than one's risk.

Thieves will still steal, and predators will still kill. The only difference is not presenting opportunity but rather challenging it.

CHAPTER 9

Scenting

Basics of Scenting

The concept of using scent as a deterrent is based on the predator's olfactory system being far superior to ours.

Many say that you must manage your attractants not to attract the predators. This statement supports the first statement's concept. It seems the major talking point to many is boneyards. Many believe that they are the biggest concern and attractant. My thought is that our cattle themselves are the attractant. Even by removing the boneyards, our true risk still remains—our cattle. My concerns are the cattle. This effort is to deter a predator's presence from them.

I spent a couple of years learning trapping skills from a retired federal trapper. The ranch I was managing was losing calves to several different species but probably the one that accounted for most of the losses was feral dogs and coyotes, canines.

We would produce a scent as an attractant. It was effective, but stink doesn't quite describe its powerful aroma. Each time you set traps, you wore the same coverings, using the scent in setting the trap, being very careful not to foul the set with an odor or mistake that gave away the set to the predator.

What I quickly realized was that it is easier to foul a set than to set an effective one.

This was the basis for choosing scent as a deterrent. If you can foul a set easier than setting an effective set, it means the predators are extremely sensitive and would be very responsive to a scent deterrent. I have written previously about the levels of fear and fear's response of fight or flight. All of which are based on instinctual reactions. The instinct of fear creates a reaction rather than a thought process. By presenting an unfamiliar scent, we engage an instinctual response.

Man-made scents are designed to mask over scents that offend us. They are powerful and economically affordable. These concentrated scents are completely foreign to the natural environment.

It is also important to keep the scent engaging the response of fear so that we engage the response of flight, simply asking the predators to move on.

In order to keep the scent engaging the response of fear, we must keep it an unsolvable riddle. In order to do that, we must prevent the predator from being aware of its placement.

Placing the scent should be done with as much thought as placing a camera or a trap set. We don't want to compromise the scent by placing it with one of nature's familiar scents or even one of man's.

Scent within the animal kingdom is powerful. A patriarch wolf will mark the boundaries of his pack's territory by marking the perimeters. He alerts other wolves, "This is mine." By scenting our area, we are simply stating, "This is ours."

Don't place it low enough that the predators can contact it.

Do not pour it on the ground.

Both of these actions give the predators an opportunity to discover where the scent is coming from. That awareness eliminates the riddle, disengaging the instinct of self-preservation and fear's response of fight or flight.

That awareness then has become a desensitizing event, creating comfort and a reason to stick around. Place the scent high in the breeze, preferably not on greenwood or sapwood nor on treated posts. The placement must allow the scent to remain a solitary scent that is strange and new. Not a combination of understandable scents that are commonly understood in nature.

Saturating a wick, in a container, preventing spillage.

I have previously written about the deterring scent being a manufactured scent and used in its concentrated form. They are affordable and readily available in any grocery store's cleaner or detergent aisle. They are completely foreign to a natural environment.

I was told about a situation that happened at a zoo. The zoo ran into a problem with its newly acquired wolves. They bunched in an outside corner of the pen and would not come to food or water. After many opinions and suggestions, someone stopped using the cleaner that the staff was washing the pens out with on a daily basis. And in a short time, the wolves were back to normal. The scent had a response, that response was fear brought on by the scent of the cleaner.

Changing the location and the scent every week to ten days, you are constantly presenting a new and unfamiliar scent, presenting an ever-changing deterrent, never allowing the predators to become accustomed to a specific scent.

When selecting a sight for placement, it is a good idea to understand your local weather. Let's say that a breeze usually comes up in the afternoon, and it usually comes from the west. The application of the scent will be much more effective if placed on the west side of the range, allowing the breeze to disperse it to the east side and across the range.

Realize that weather isn't always consistent, so applications must be applied within your parameters around a half to one mile apart.

Moisture via rain only reactivates aging scents and presents an onslaught of scent deterrents that were previously applied. Drought dries the scent and weakens its distribution. Staying on a scheduled routine is recommended.

When we look at our range and we are determining placements, it's important to understand the geographical parameters and how and where predators are traveling. If you are in a corridor where the predators are traveling to a destination, such as a water source or another attraction, it may require a staggered placement to encourage them, seeking an alternate route.

Man-made roads do work as game trails. They're often placed where they are placed because an engineer found it to be the easiest and shortest route to a destination. The same principle works for the predators.

The roads also have an attractant value to the predators. People being people throw or lose items from their vehicles—maybe a partial piece of sandwich or a beer can. The vehicles also supply another item, roadkill. These are all attractants to predators, making the roads a very commonly used predator route.

Game trails that cross man-made roads are an intersection of travel patterns for the predators. What they sense at these intersections determines their direction. If you determine where these intersections are in relation to the range that you are trying to deter presence on, you can place a scent marker for the trail that detours the predator from your direction.

The roads are an attractant, but remember that we place an attractant in a trap set. And that trap is easily fouled by a deterring scent. Deterring scents have a reaction of instinctual responses which overpower simple desires.

The most important factor to deterrents is not allowing them to become familiar. By allowing familiarity, you desensitize a reaction. Such repetition (not changing the scent routinely) engages desensitization, and it is the basis for habituation.

If you can't effectively reapply scent within a seven to ten-day window of application, don't choose scenting as a deterrent.

It is important to keep the scent placements ever-changing—both in the placement's location and the actual scent. If you used a fabric softener last, apply a cleaner the next time.

I don't purchase gallons. I prefer the smaller bottles offered at the discount stores. It may be that I'm a cheapskate but more importantly is that the supply runs out quickly, and I can change to another scent direction. Keeping the placements ever-changing, fresh, and unfamiliar to the predators.

Sometimes the placements seem to be hindered by not having a reasonable spot to apply the scent. One of the most common problems is the only thing I have to place scent on is a barbwire fence. That fence's braces are treated posts or pipe braces having no clean wood or anything for the scent to soak into.

Although I prefer a higher placement, the fence will be used rather than placing no deterrent at all. I will use a wick that will hold the scent. That wick is a strip of fabric, an old sock, a handkerchief, a strip of old Levi's—anything that can be wrapped around the top wire. I like the strip to be about four inches wide and eight to ten inches long. I like to cut a split lengthwise on one end, then stabbing the other end on a barb, and wrapping it itself on the wire, then using the split end to tie the wick.

By presoaking the wick lightly in the scent deterrent before wrapping it onto the wire, you eliminate the chance of overapplication and spillage, presenting an unsolvable riddle.

Scenting with a wick

Upon the reapplication, don't pour the new deterrent on the old wick but leave the old wick so it has the opportunity to be reactivated in a rain event. Apply a new wick for the new application, placing it approximately half to one mile away from the other scent.

The wick method can also be used if only live trees or brushes exist. The best item I have found is that sock that lost its mate or cheap socks purchased at the discount store. Place a wrapped-up scented wick inside the sock and tie the sock in the green tree, hanging, not touching the brush or the tree.

These are both options to place the scent deterrents.

Placing scent from a mustang colt.

By placing a scent deterrent for a while, my observation is that I have noticed a significant reduction in tracks and scat.

Another thing I have observed is the change in avian presence. It seems as if magpies, ravens, and buzzards have been absent from the areas where I have been presenting the deterrent. Some avian species seem to have a symbiotic relationship with predators. It seems as if those birds operate as scouts for the predators. A beacon that says to the predators, "Come here."

While demonstrating a howling wolf to a group, we soon had a response. The response was ravens with several appearing and staying at the location for a brief time.

I don't believe in coincidences, especially in animal behavior. I believe more in the probability that a response is a reaction to an action. We just fit the word coincidences in because we didn't see or connect the action to the reaction.

A thought is that scenting has deterred the predator's presence, and by doing so, we have also deterred the avian presence. Although we are dealing with our specific range and those specific parameters, the avian absence poses a question of how far are we deterring presence.

The wolf that came to California, the famous OR-7, was from the northeastern corner of Oregon. He was trapped and collared there. His response was to line out to a new country—a response of flight that brought him to California. Did the trapping and collaring engage a response of fear, or was his journey to California simply a coincidence?

The degree of a response to a stimulus is itself unknown. We don't know the degree of fear that we present. Scenting, though, has been an effective solution for deterring presence.

Scent Deterrents Are Effective

Fall is a busy time. Livestock distributions are condensing as the natural resources are at the end of the growing season. As hunting seasons are winding down, so is the available hunting aftermath for the predators.

The predators, as well as the livestock, are beginning to condense because both are seeking a more available food source.

Because of the presence of the pajaroello tick and the cattle's response to foothill abortion, I have two calving seasons. The spring calving herd is more susceptible to foothill abortion than the fall calving herd.

The fall is the season when most of the foothill abortions occur. The third trimester of pregnancy is the timing of the abortion. An opportune time for the predators as their proximity to the cattle condenses.

Such an attractant brings predators closer and jeopardizes the healthy fall calves.

When a cow aborts, we make the effort to graft another calf onto the mother cow to help mitigate the financial loss.

One of the tricks to getting the mother cow to accept the new live calf is to fool her into accepting that the calf is the same calf that she aborted. We skin the dead calf and tie the hide onto the live calf so that the mother will accept it. This is called grafting.

After a brief time, the hide is removed, and the mother and her newly adopted calf are returned to the herd. By grafting, the cow moves from the spring herd and into the falls.

Disposing of the hide is a necessity because the decomposing hide is an attractant to predators.

In the grafting process, I apparently lost track of the hide, and apparently, one of my dogs absconded with it.

My first realization of a problem was the magpies that I began seeing. I spent a few hours searching for a problem. But at this time, I was still unaware of the missing hide.

Ravens soon followed, and then a large number of howling coyotes soon moved into close proximity to the cattle's location.

Unable to find a problem, I applied a round of scent deterrents. The coyotes were gone within the day. I still was scratching my head over what was drawing them.

The next morning, when I was driving out to feed some first calf heifers, one of my younger dogs jumped into the truck, carrying his prize—the graft calves adopting cape, the missing hide.

As I have said before, I don't believe in coincidences, especially when it comes to animal behavior.

Although the magpies are not a predator, I believe their actions act as an alert or as scouts for the predators. Their presence alerts nearby predators of opportunity. I believe that buzzards and ravens are also incorporated into this mix.

Keeping the area free of attractants may seem to be a minor detail, but if allowed, the coyotes would quickly consume that dead abortion and not be satisfied because of the lack of food volume that it provided. They would certainly have food on their mind and continue looking for opportunities. That opportunity would be the healthy fall calves.

Deterring presence is the first step in deterring conflict. Although unintentional, the graft hide was an active attractant, and by placing the scent deterrent, it proved again that scenting is effective in deterring predators, mitigating the risk to the healthy calves.

CHAPTER 10

Monitoring

Monitoring Update

The *predator awareness* training that was applied in 2016 on National Forest allotments was a successful effort. The *stockmanship skill* of *predator awareness training* was not used or applied in the off-season to the two ranches that were on the USFS allotments. The purpose of that was to return the cattle and wait to hear of a possible response of handling issues or problems. None were reported. Another issue was to measure the training's retention among the cattle. After seven months of layoff with no *predator awareness stockmanship* being used, the cattle returned to the forest allotments, and predator monitoring began again. The response of each of the two ranches that are on forestry permits had very similar results.

The observations of 2017 were limited to one day per week. The reason for the reduced time allotted was the removal of financial assistance of an NGO. The ranchers' concerns of wolf presence resulted in the ranchers carrying the efforts on their own. The result of that was no time for training updates. The time allotted was used to monitor predators' presence and apply scent and update scent deterrents.

The first contacts with the cattle were in July and showed that the cattle appeared to be maintaining the herd group posture. Slight pressure tests were applied and with good results. The cattle grouped and stood their ground.

The summer months this year were warmer than usual. As stated in the *wolf migration* paper, the *microclimate theory* posed warm weather for wolf presence and possibly other mammal predators' pressures in these locations. This lack of predators may have contributed to the following lapses in *predator awareness training retention*.

The behavior that was observed in the herds that did not receive continued *predator awareness training* updates was that the cattle began to show a steady decline in *herd awareness* and more frequent observations of individualized grazing. When the *pressure test* was applied, flight often seemed to have no purpose or direction. Individual livestock did not seek the comfort and security of the herd group and seemed too often stay individualized—an apparent loss of *herd awareness*. The reason for the training fading may be the lack of predators or the training simply may have a shelf life. The end of the last year's training seems to have lost its effectiveness at eight to nine months. The facts are that without continued *predator awareness* updates in training, the herd group's defensive posture of *predator awareness training* may fade away.

The ranchers that continued updates and *predator awareness stockmanship skills*, their livestock had the appearance to be more content and had them remaining and grazing with *herd awareness*, and the *pressure tests* still resulted in the defensive posture of *predator awareness* although these cattle were in Oregon and had close proximity to wolves, which may have aided in the posturing of the herd groups. With the training updates, the cattle appeared to stay calmer and appeared to graze and loaf in herd groups.

Observations: The *predator awareness training* is intended to promote a calm defensive herd posture. In observing cattle in proximity to one of the cooperating ranches in Oregon, several groups of neighboring cattle in surrounding areas appeared to be highly sensitive and flighty. This condition remained for several weeks. The project cattle that had been trained in *predator awareness* appeared to have a tighter *herd awareness* posture threw this time. Although the trained cattle did not show any signs of stress or heightened anxiety, the speculation is that there had been some type of stressful pressure in the area, possibly predators.

Conclusion: *Predator awareness stockmanship* requires a maintenance program. The effort of continuing the practice of proactive *stockmanship* is a change in all your livestock handling activities and all promote the herd response of the herd being the livestock's safe zone.

Comments: Over several years, observations of livestock and their geographic dispositions show a difference in grazing and loafing patterns. Cattle that are in areas of nonpredator pressure show a natural looser grouping. Although cattle that are in known predator areas may also show disbursed patterns, they are often seen in tight herd groups. With the network of relayed sightings of predators, although just hearsay, the sightings confirm a predator's pressure creates the defensive posture of herding. The ranchers by establishing the livestock's posture of herding prior to the predators establishing the same reaction diminish the risk of individualization and promote a calm herd action and create a herd response that makes handling an easier and calmer management practice.

Monitoring and Scenting—Part 2

A monitoring program is an effort to determine predatory risks of any given area by determining whether there is a predator presence. The monitoring effort needs to be maintained on a regular basis. It would be convenient if the area being monitored could be covered in one day. But most of the time, the area will need to be monitored in sections. The effort should be a routine that puts you back to the first starting section within seven to ten days of the last visit.

There are many variables that enter into developing a program. Risks can be present in any terrain at any time that livestock are present. But there are times the risks are not worth the effort of monitoring. The predators require things also. Certain predators may tolerate certain terrain, temperatures, and water availability while others may not. By examining the geography, water supply, and salt grounds, along with game trails, cow trails, and roads, we can understand the fundamental travel routes of a given range.

The geography of California dictates cattle presence from one season to the next. Those seasonal movements of livestock correspond to most of the predators and game. The main factor is the temperature and the presence of attractants. The cattle and the game are the attractants.

There is a lot said about attractants. Because there are so many things that can be considered attractants, there are quite a few who want to focus on the one that is popular at the time. As of 2019 in California, it seems to be boneyards. This requires a little California history. Since the conquistadors first established the first missions for Spain in the late 1500s, California has had a cattle presence. In fact, California's first industry was the hide and tallow trade for Spain. The first currency was a cowhide. At present, California is the fourth largest cattle producer in the United States. That is a cattle population in California of 5.2 million head (Beef2Live).

The national death loss is 1 percent. That's fifty-two thousand head of cattle that die naturally within California's state lines each year. Most of the rendering plants were closed for environmental reasons from the 1960s through the 1970s. The ranchers were forced to deal with those dead stock themselves. It is against regulations to bury or burn, so the piles were the only legal solutions.

Let's run some numbers: fifty-two thousand head at an average cow weight of 1,500 pounds is 78 million pounds per year, which when broken down to semiloads is 1,560 semiloads per year. Times fifty years is 78,000 semi loads that we are talking about. Let's say that one semi would cost $2,500 to load and clean up a boneyard. That is a cleanup cost of $195 million. To protect a product that is worth $12 million, and if all boneyards are removed, there are still many more attractants such as roadkills.

In developing solutions, it would be my opinion that removing attractants is at best a long-term project. It is also my belief that the wolf is a permanent fixture on the west coast. I believe that the best solution for wolf presence is to assume he is here and protect our cattle.

Roads. They need to be monitored for the presence of scat. Canids often choose roadways to defecate. These can be gravel or paved. Game trails will often align with well-travel roads with high traffic. These aligning trails are often traveled by predators who monitor the well-trafficked roadways for roadkill. These game trails will often cross or intersect the roadways. That area is a priority checkpoint for tracks.

Scat characteristics. Canids families will have different size scats. Wolves being the largest, and foxes being the smallest. But the characteristics of the canid scat will all be the same. Pinched to a point at least on one end, the canid will choose an open space or sometimes place it on an elevated spot.

Felines, such as lions, can actually resemble a wolf's scat. But the feline species bury theirs. Feline's choice spots are often loose types of soils or hummus. The challenge is recognizing those loose types of venues and then recognizing the buried piles.

Bear's scats are segmented. They don't have the pinched taper such as canine but have a broken flat end. Bears are omnivores, so the scats consisting of cellulosic material are often found and left for easy identification. But bear's meat scats seem to disappear rather quickly, possibly as a protein source for other wildlife or smaller carnivorous.

Dogs, either *stock dogs* or *predator awareness* dogs, are good to have along on monitoring circles, as they often can be the alert and key to finding wildlife signs such as scats.

Evaluating. Scats are a key component in determining whether livestock losses have occurred. Besides presence, we need to check scats for herd losses to predators. Sometimes the clues that the scat reveals can be the first signal to a problem. For example, maybe you find a coyote scat that contains some red cow hair, but your herd is predominately black. Your neighbors are predominantly red. The clue lends a suggestion of where to search for the problem—your neighbor's areas. But possibly, you find some neighbor's cows in your area. That, too, is a possible sign of predatory pressures. Even though the scat was determined to be from a coyote, it may have just been clean up of a kill by an apex predator. The neighbor's cows may be moved due to predatory pressures. Evaluating is putting pieces together to understand the predatory presence.

Hair. It is a marker that can easily describe the predator's diet and behavior. Hair remains undigested and retains its color. It is merely the diagnosis of what prey victim it came from. By using your boot and stepping down then sliding to the side, you smear the scat into a flat plate that can then be examined.

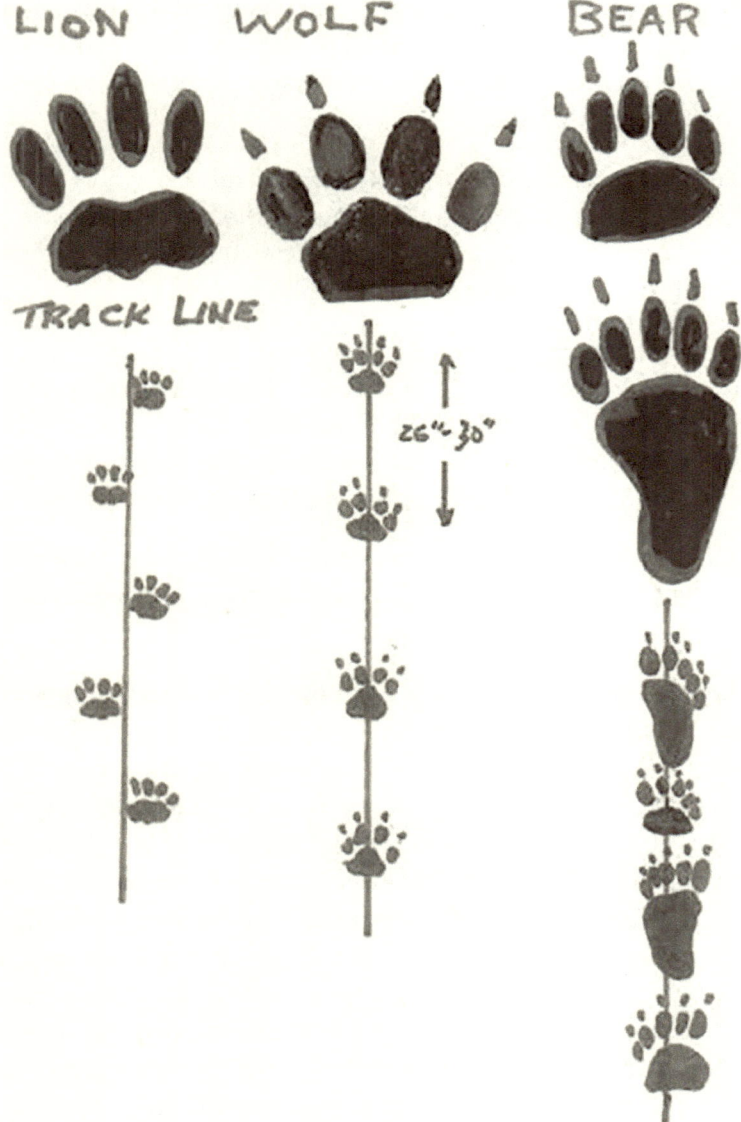

Tracks. Tracking requires a readable pallet for identification. Dry-powered dirt or moist dirt is best for track identification. Although ideal tracking conditions seldom occur, there are characteristics that can determine species. Canids are all the same print—they just escalate in size. Foxes being the smallest then Coyotes and finally wolves. Felines follow the same way, bob-cats to lions only differentiated by their size.

Determining what created the tract in canid species, there are some distinctive characteristics that we can apply. But first, individual tracts "one footprint" should not attest to any one species but attest to several possibilities. Guessing at one footprint is just that—guessing.

If we apply a number to each foot, the left front being number 1, the right front being number 2, the left hind being number 3, and finally, the right hind is number 4, we then can examine each gate of travel and understand what we are looking at. If we are looking at a walk, the cadence would be 1, 4, 2, 3.

If we are tracking a dog, the left hind would be on the same left line as the left front: 1 and 3. And of course, 2 and 4 would be on their own line. The left feet would be on the left and the right feet on the right. Both sides would have a void center space between the left side and the right side. Livestock, horses, deer, and dogs all travel in this way. Wild canids are a bit different in their movement. The cadence will remain the same 1, 4, 2, 3. But the line traveled will not have a right or left side. The line traveled will be one line with no center void to it. No left or right side. All the feet would be on the same line. It should be understood that the line at a walk may wander a bit, zigzagging here and there. The pace that wild canids prefer is a dog trot. At this trot, they can cover long distances relatively quickly. It seems to be their preferred gate for travel. At this gate, the tracts for wild canids will appear in one continuous line, giving them a very distinctive character to their track identification.

Signs. It must be taken into account. Cattle that appear nervous or are not in their proper place are signs that should wave a red flag. Game in areas that are not normally visited by that game. The lack of other predators such as coyotes should immediately create the thought: wolf. Wolves will prey on coyotes, and coyotes will leave an area when they are present. Birds, such as ravens and magpies, will follow wolves looking for the next meal.

Markers. When monitoring, I may add in additional areas that may show something questionable. But as part of monitoring, these routine trails I will *set markers* that I check. They are placed somewhere that I routinely pass. These *markers* are old boots or an empty aluminum can. They are placed as prizes, so to speak, to be taken to pups as toys. Sometimes the hunting adult takes such things to a rendezvous site. If the markers are missing, I look much closer for a sign, such as tracts. Pups of the canine species love to chew on cans and shoes. Seeing such accumulated junk should alert you to a possible rendezvous or den sight.

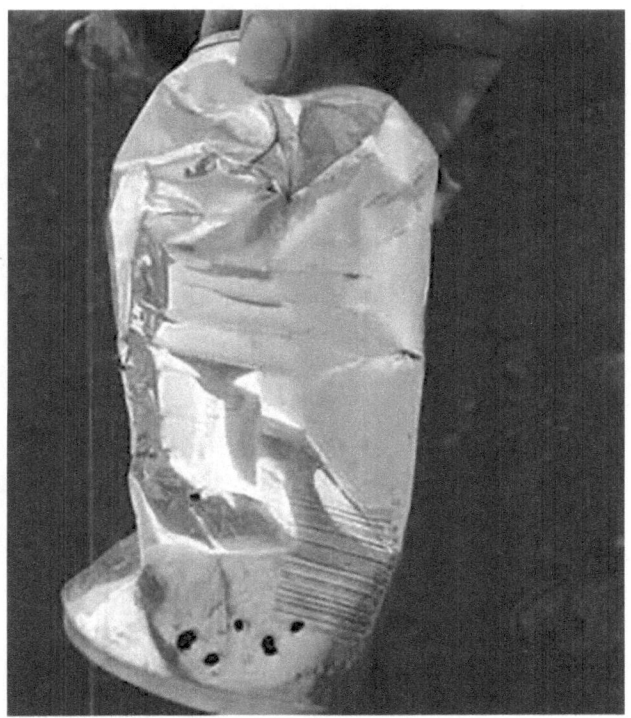

All our time is valuable. But when you are out monitoring, take the time to look at trash. Often, there is a sign of presence within that area.

Camera placements. It should be on trails that have probable destination spots. These cow trails are often combined corridors of travel for game and livestock. They help monitor the cattle's disposition and predatory presence. A destination would be water, salt or minerals, or open tracts of abundant feed. The placement of the camera should take those routes into consideration. But other placements may include your boneyard or dead animals that may not be retrievable from the range. Actual trash piles left by campers or hunters or unexplained piles and even the hunter's campsites after they have left. All those places can be an attractant. Do not place attractants in areas where you are trying to deter presence. Don't buy a scent to place to get some good pictures.

I like camera placements to be closer to the ground than some like. It helps me find more cover to disguise the camera placements. I don't like a predator to be able to see the camera when approaching it. I prefer that it had already passed its location, and I got a few shots of it walking away. But that requires a one-way trail, and that's not reality. The effort then becomes a side shot. That's been the best placement for me.

Scenting. People say that human presence is an effective deterrent. We as humans tend to think of that statement as if we are actually standing there. Human presence to a canine is scent. Just as hounds can track by scent, wild species can determine the human presence in the same manner.

So what is human scent? When we think of human scent, we think of the scents that offend us—perspiration, flatulence, and bad breath. They are our natural scents. But they have been with humans since the beginning, and I believe that predators are confident and understand those particular human scents.

What is new and strange to the predators is the manufactured scents that we make to mask over the scents that offend us. Scents that we are comfortable with are masking agents—manufactured scents. They come in concentrated deodorizing.

By placing these scent deterrents undiluted in strategic placements, they have a powerful suggestion of human presence. These scents that are soothing to us are quite an unknown and unsettling scent to predators. These scents have a wide selection of purposes and are economically affordable. They include laundry detergents to floor cleaners, deodorizers, fabric softeners—the list is large.

Apply the scents high in the breeze and then reapply in seven to ten days with a new and different scent to avoid the scents becoming commonplace. The scent always presents a new and uncomfortable question of human presence.

Predator awareness and *scenting* take into account one of the strongest instincts in all living animals, self-preservation. Self preservations response is fear. When we present an unknown, it generates the reaction of self-preservation and tells the predator to move on.

Deterring presence. The response of our cattle reacting to a *predator's presence* and applying the *standing solution* and seeking the *defensive posture of the herd group* is the second line of defense. Both efforts when combined make an effective deterrent.

Changing bad behavior. In my younger years, I believed that problematic animals, such as a horse or a dog or even livestock, were just a challenge. I had the opportunity to work with and buy some very good quality animals at bargain prices or even had owners who would pay me to work with their problems.

I had quite a few horses that fell into this category.

I had a red dun gelding that had been left as a stud and untouched until he was five. A friend of mine was paid by the owner to capture, geld, and ride this horse and find a market for him.

He contacted me, so I soon owned this gelding. I owned him for about five years. This horse had seen many miles and doctored many head of cattle. But I was the only one who could use or come in contact with this horse.

His demeanor was just too nasty to risk someone else's safety. Although this gelding could accomplish any ranch task and cover tuff country on back-to-back days, his real threat was being around him on the ground rather than working upon him.

His feet were untouchable. In trying, that effort put that horse into a fight mode that was actually scary. I had a vet tell me that he could give the horse a sedative to successfully allow someone to work with his feet.

I told the vet that I would give it a try and set up an appointment. I planned on doing the work myself but called another friend who shoed for a living to assist.

The day came, and the vet filled a syringe. I had secured the horse to an unbreakable post in the corrals and let the vet work his magic. The horse pinned his ears and raised a hind leg as if telling the vet, "Come on, I dare you." After a few efforts and me shortening his lead rope, the vet moved into the horse's neck and put the needle into the horse's jugular.

The jab of the needle sent this horse into a full-blown attack mode. The horse pinned the vet against the fence and tried his darnedest to cow kick the vet while he had the vet pinned.

We were attempting through all this to get the horse's attention away from the vet. The horse finally broke the halter and moved to the end of the corrals. We had the vet up and starting over the fence as the horse was coming to administer his revenge on the vet. The vet wasn't over the fence yet, and the horse bit a leg of his coveralls and dragged him back into his domain.

The vet was yelling and crawling, looking for an escape route. There was a built-in hay manger that the vet made it into. Our efforts also had success, as we got a rope on this horse and secured it to a post, limiting the horse's pursuit. We soon had this horse secured and turned our attention to the vet who was still in the manger.

There were pieces of coveralls spread across the corral. The vet had taken a few serious kicks or strikes but didn't think anything was broken. As we assisted him, he was conveying his adamant thoughts about my horse.

As long as I owned this horse, there was a standing offer of $100 to anyone who could shoe him. There were a few tries, but no one ever claimed the prize.

I continued to work this horse, not allowing anyone but myself to be around him.

When you stepped on this horse, it required staying in front of his elbow, lest he would reach you with a hind leg. I have never ridden a horse that when walking could reach up with a hind and kick your heel with his toe. It made the use of spurs dangerous as the horse could do serious damage. But as sensitive as this horse was, he never required spurs.

I had a pasture where I occasionally weaned calves and kept my saddle horses. I had a fella stop several times to ask about this horse, as this gelding could hold his own in most conformation classes.

My response was he's not for sale. After his third request, I started to tell him why he didn't want him. I didn't hold any cards. I laid them all down. He left his number if I changed my mind.

Two weeks had passed, and he caught me dropping horses off at this pasture after a tough day. He pealed out $2,500 in cash. I told him that I didn't believe that he and this horse would be a good match.

He told me that he was an experienced charro and liked such a horse.

I helped put the horse in the trailer.

About a year later, another man stopped who was the buyer's brother and informed me that the horse was put down after injuring his brother.

As I had said, there were several horses that were problematic.

Another horse, a mare, had the problem of rearing, and then at the pinnacle of the rear, the horse would jump higher and land on her back. All this began as the rider was about to cast his leg over.

I was fortunate to have access to many quality horsemen, many of which told me to chicken the horse. One man that was a retired cow boss for a large historical Nevada ranch told me he had experience with this bad behavior. His solution was a tie-down and a rope that went between both the front and hind legs and secured to the tail.

The rope had approximately a three to four-inch gap between the horse's belly when the horse was standing still. He told me when I stepped up and she began the rear, the rope would pull her tail, launching her forward.

The first few mounts were like riding a rocket, but she proved she could really run. The horse turned into a pretty nice team roping horse. I rode her with that solution throughout the time I owned her, often getting comments and many solutions to be able to do away with the belly rope.

Again, someone wanted this mare, and after telling the buyer about the required belly rope, he took her home to try her out. After about ten days, he assured me that the horse and he were a good fit. Apparently, after a few ropings and getting razzed by other ropers, his efforts changed into doing away with such a silly device as the belly rope.

In a practice session, he placed a traditional tie-down that secured itself to the cinch, allowing the mare to rear in the box, pinning him between her and the butt rail, causing serious injuries.

Problem behavioral issues can be dealt with, but just as with addictions or alcoholism, the problem can resurface if a continuation of the solution is abandoned or the effort in the performance of the solution weakens.

My point of these stories is that a problem often has a solution if we are willing to apply the effort. The alternative is to live with the problem or remove ourselves from the situation.

We have to realize that the predators are just that—predators. Nothing can change that. Adapting to working with its behaviors is an effort we must achieve to continue to operate our business.

CHAPTER 11

Conclusion

In the ten years of developing these techniques, my efforts went from five losses per year to only one loss in ten years. The effort is about our interactions with the animals within our everyday world. By engaging proactively, we can present to our stock, as well as to the predators, an alternative to the presence and confrontation that is so destructive to our bottom line as well as to our stock.

Fear

Fear is a response rather than an instinct. If we can address instinct, the responses can be favorable to our interests and deterring presence. That same engagement of fear can be used to promote a solution to predatory encounters for our stock, which is the standing solution.

The Herd

The fact that cattle are herd animals doesn't mean that all cattle that are in a group equal a defensive posture. Cattle group for a multitude of reasons, the herd's defensive posture through the years and the absence of predators has faded the response and takes an effort to reestablish.

As with any skill, one wants to become proficient. Such proficiency takes effort and practice. The defensive posture of the herd group is no different. If left to the predators, the predators will establish the response that suits their objective.

Monitoring

Monitoring, rather than being a scheduled chore, should become an everyday awareness of our surroundings.

Scent Deterrent

By placing an ever-changing scent deterrent, we present the first line of defense. By engaging a predator's primary sensory perception with an unknown, we create a riddle that poses a question. That unresolvable riddle creates an uncomfortable place for the predator to be. Touching the predator on an instinctual level and summoning fear's responses.

Benefits

By developing our skills as a stockman, we can develop a solution that promotes comfort and a sense of well-being for the stock that we work with.

The effort of predator awareness is not about changing an animal's behavioral characteristics but understanding and working with its behavioral tendencies.

Predators are just that, predators—they're opportunists. Mitigating risks changes nothing other than one's risk.

2015 USFWS Grant Paper
Training Cattle with Predator Awareness

Mark Coats

TRAINING CATTLE

Predator awareness

In 2011, the wolf designated as OR-7 entered Siskiyou County, California. In November 2015, the first probable wolf and livestock conflict occurred. The presence of the *wolf*, which is protected by law and the Endangered Species Act, has created concerns for the ranching community. Through research and practice, the method of *predator awareness* was created. Even with successful performance, we are dealing with an apex predator and make no guarantees for any solutions offered. Our ranges of Northern California and Southern Oregon are unlike the ranges of other areas that can support the herds existing in one continuous group. Our ranges lend themselves to smaller groups spread over greater distances. That requires our cattle to a group in smaller numbers, and those groups must react as a defensive herd, which can be an effective deterrent to the predator's presence.

Predators are an expense to the bottom line of any *ranching* operation. How to mitigate this risk is the purpose of this paper. Predators are why herds exist and cattle are herd animals (Mooring and Hart 1992). The herd is a defensive posture livestock use to avoid predation. Ranching and management practices have caused some of our livestock to lose the herding reaction and become desirable prey to predators (Grandin and Deesing 2014). Many of our practices and studies are made by separating individual livestock from the herd, but very little is done to return the individual to its herd group and promote herding. Our objective is to reinstill those herd instincts among livestock production and to create a reaction that resembles *musk* ox or *bison*.

The beef industry encourages low-stress livestock handling, but low-stress livestock handling is a tool used when humans are dealing with management practices and livestock. There are those promoting it as a deterrent to predation. It is not a deterrent. If humans are present, the wolf is not. Predators are a concern when humans are not present, such as on open ranges and large pastures, or on feeding grounds that border predator habitats, such as wooded or forestry interfaces.

Breeding and creating meaner cattle is not the solution. That only creates individuals who want to chase and fight the predators, establishing an individualized chase sequence, fitting very nicely into the predator's methods of hunting. Creating *predator awareness* first begins with understanding predator-prey relations or the hunt, capture, and consumption of the prey, which have their own dynamics. Our concern will be on wolf/livestock confrontation although other predatory mammals may be deterred by this *stockmanship approach*. There are four predator species of concern in these areas: coyotes, mountain lions, black bears, and wolves. With camera monitoring, it was apparent that the livestock herd instincts had changed. Cattle monitored were not seen as individuals only as groups, only additional cattle that were brought from other areas and had not received any training showed individualization. Cameras support the fact that the herd training that the livestock received remained intact when humans were not present and the trained cattle remained in herd groups. Through camera surveillance, the *predator awareness* training created a behavior in cattle that showed they moved and grazed in herds.

A predator finding prey must select, single out, pursue, and capture its prey. Wolves generally chase their prey as a pack and can pursue them for great distances. Even when wolves hunt as individuals, they still chase and run their prey. By removing the pursuit or chase, we are interrupting the hunting sequence. Our goal is to establish *predator awareness* that creates a reaction from our livestock to seek other cattle, group together, and stand, not running or pursuing the predator. Doing this will create a safe, calm defiant herd stance, and we remove stress and the losses associated with the stress of the chase.

With calm resolve and deterred predator individualization, and by removing the chase sequence, we are discouraging the predator's pressure, and we are interrupting the predator-prey relationship. It is an effective management solution that can be integrated into modern-day beef production with *stockmanship*. There are economic values of cattle that react to their environment with confidence and contentment. Promoting cattle well-being with sound management can add to the bottom line. This deterrent is a low-cost producer-based solution.

This *stockmanship* approach has been developed and worked on since 2012. It was applied to three cooperating ranches in the grazing season of 2016, where predators and livestock were monitored with trail camera placements. These ranches are all commercial cow/ calf producers in Northern California and Southern Oregon. The ranches consisted of three calving dates, fall, spring, and year-round. The ranches encompassed two US forestry permits, nine private leases, and approximately nine hundred mother cows and replacements. There were no losses due to predation. The training that was performed on two of the participating ranches was started on two US forest grazing permits with no previous training in the livestock. The third ranch had been working on developing this training skill since 2012. Through the livestock training of one full-time rider and one part-time assistant and two dogs, they accomplished the *predator awareness* training of all the livestock in all the areas.

There are three components to this *stockmanship* approach. The first is the *standing solution*, where the cattle are encouraged to group as a herd and not run or flee, to stand calm in a group, not fighting, pursuing, or individualizing themselves away from the herd's safety and its *standing solution*. The *standing solution* is to discourage flight or the act of running away as an individual. The second is *herd awareness*. This is a loose grouping of cattle that are aware of where the group is at all times. When cattle are confronted with pressure or a stressful situation they are aware of the herd's location and react with movement toward the group. The final component is *predator awareness*, which is the reaction of herding into a defensive posture to deter a predator's presence in a herd group. The defensive posture is the herd itself. Encouraging and training cattle to react to a predator's presence by seeking the herd for comfort and security is the key to *predator awareness.*

By promoting and establishing livestock reactions to pressure by herding and grouping in the *standing solution* cattle can deter predators on their own without human interaction. This training of cattle invokes other beneficial behavior such as handling ease and herd gentleness. This can aid in the ability to gather in a rough country with less labor, calmly and safely, and with better success and results. There are also financial benefits. Less stress creates better conception rates, higher gains, and less depredation. This is a producer-based solution to an apex predator involving management decisions that are measured in benefits to livestock production and quality of life, which can lower inputs and have higher rewards than other deterrents. This deterrent focuses on our livestock. It does not focus on the *wolf.*

The cattle pictured here are grazing with *herd awareness.* The photo on the left shows the proper cattle grouping before stress was introduced. While walking through the pasture to reach the cattle for inspection, a routine that is usually performed on horseback, the cattle perceived stress and reacted with the response that they were trained with. The photo on the right shows the stance is divergent, and they have found security with the herd. The goal of *predator awareness* is achieved with calm resolve.

This management tool is practiced and applied long before it is required and is continually practiced and promoted. It is in effect a new livestock handling procedure. We are trying to create a cattle herd that reacts to pressure. The harder the push, the firmer they stand, creating a herd that stops and cannot be pushed, chased, or individualized. This method establishes the *standing solution* to a predator's presence *does not create a handling problem.* Low-stress handling is still encouraged and necessary. *Predator awareness* training actually creates a well-mannered herd and instills quieter and gentler handling responses.

Many daily ranching activities encourage cattle to flee or individualize themselves. Tasks not associated with livestock and their handling, such as irrigating, feeding, or monitoring livestock or passing through the field can create movement. "Movement is intentional, not random." As an example, you are beginning herd training and you are crossing a field and in your path is a cow lying chewing her cud in the direction that you want to proceed on. Traditionally, we would just walk on, and the cow would have to move. By making your way around her, you begin the process, letting her know that it is okay to stand, and the response of standing instead of movement is begun. These actions, though small, are part of creating the *standing solution*. The trainings that will follow are all *pressure and release*, with the release being the reward when a calm *standing solution* is achieved. We are redirecting our attention to stopping and standing cattle before movement occurs.

If movement is created unintentionally, try to resolve that movement into a stop or pause. For example, the back door of the shop might be close to a water trough. When leaving the shop, you surprise some stock watering, and they flee in response. You have no way to react to stop them other than a soft-toned call. Try a quiet call to see if you can create a pause in their flight. Try a call that resembles the sound of a calf (*urrrr*), effectively stopping the movement rather than pushing.

Canis lupus, the wolf, that has entered our area, and the timber wolf is a canine. In order to expose our livestock to stress that resembles the wolf and his predatory skills, we will require dogs. These dogs' primary skills will be stopping and creating the *standing solution* (see diagram 1). The dog's role also can be defined as a pseudo-predator. It is understood that much of our industry opposes the presence of dogs, but the dogs can help create a preconditioned response from our livestock to prevent depredation. If you currently use stock dogs, it may be easier and better served to add a dog for the *predator awareness* training rather than retraining your dogs.

The beginning of the training depends on your cattle's dog tolerance. If your cattle are familiar with dogs or if they fight and chase dogs without correction, that is a recipe for predator depredation. You must take the time to accustom the livestock to dog presence before training begins. If you already use dogs, but it is in a more traditional movement, it will be a challenge to change the communication between your dog the cattle and you.

When a dog is chosen to be the *predator awareness* training dog, his job is specific to that effort. Don't use the *predator awareness* training dog in combination as a stock dog, and don't use your stock dogs for training of *predator awareness*. One task seeks movement, and one promotes standing. The combination only confuses the effort and the livestock's reaction. Chasing, pushing, and barking dogs are not a benefit to the goal of *predator awareness* and the *standing solution*. The desired dog is predominantly a strong, quick heading dog, quick to stop cattle, and has a soft responsive handle, traditional stock dogs that are used to move cattle and promote movement are not what we are seeking. Our objective is to achieve the grouping, herding, and *standing solution*. Dogs that are trained to encourage stopping instead of directing or pushing.

When you are walking or riding through cattle without your dog, there should be a different response than with your dog from your cattle. As you move without your dog, the response should be a calm carefree attitude, even reflecting a relaxed grazing mode reaction to your presence. With the dog's presence, the desired response should be heads-up alertness, and you should notice a slow but steady grouping, bunching, or herding. This is the beginning of predator awareness.

There are some stock dog breeds that are strong and efficient in shedding. The act of separating an animal from the herd, singling the animal out away from the herd. This is a very usable quality in our goal of establishing herd calmness. By using the shedding method, we can encourage that the most stressful place is away from the herd and the calmest place is with the herd. When an individual animal is away from the herd, there is pressure and stress, returning to the herd relieves the pressure and promotes herd calmness. This is otherwise known as pressure and release (see diagram 4).

By controlling the shed and moving to the inside, instead of the normal position of simply returning the stray to the herd on the pressure point of the outside, you are able to position yourself between the individual cow and the herd. By sending your dog forward to the head, the dog is turning the individual cow for a return to the herd, and you are in position to block the return. Blocking the return creates a greater training opportunity. This opportunity promotes the herd as a place of security and comfort. Blocking reaffirms that the herd is where that animal needs to be. This method is to instill that being away and individualized from the herd creates pressure on our dog and the trainer. Upon the release and it returns to the herd, it establishes an awareness of a solution to that stress and pressure, the return to the herd.

The beginning of training is preferred to be done in a confined field with parameters although it can be performed on ranges and large pastures that require more miles. The larger areas will require replacements for tired horses and tired dogs. Starting in a smaller field allows better and slower control. The goal of training herd awareness to deter predators, is that the cattle when confronted, seek each other and bind as a herd. The primary goal is to stop cattle from leaving the herd (Diagram 1), to not to individualize themselves for any reason, but to find safety and comfort with other cattle. Which will promote our objective of cattle learning that the herd is their best defense against predators. Not fleeing or fighting but standing calmly with attention and resolve (Diagram 5).

The type of cattle you are working with will also affect your efforts in the beginning. All the classes of cattle react differently to pressure. If you are dealing with weaned calves or yearlings, the preferred dog would go forward wider with more distance between the cattle and himself, and the effort to stop will take more attempts than it will with dry-bred cows (diagram 1). Once you have stopped the cattle and they have stood, removing pressure, the day's goal has been achieved. Do not continue that day. As humans, one of our animal training mistakes is to repeat an action to enjoy the result, but the repetition only confuses the effort in the animal's mind, and they don't connect to the reward, only to more punishment. The reward for the pressure is the release.

Instruction

The primary goal is that cattle stop and stand. We must understand that the predator's pressures are life versus death for our livestock. When a stressful situation confronts our livestock, they must react by herding and applying the *standing solution*. The flight and fleeing as individuals is not an acceptable response from our livestock. We create flight and movement to simulate a predator's pressures, which creates the opportunity to train our livestock that the herd is a safe and calm place. Running or chasing our livestock or even running around them defeats the efforts of the training. Leave the chasing and running to our assistant the dog. The dog's purpose is to simulate a predator's presence. As the trainer, our goal is to promote calmness, herding, and the *standing solution.*

Move your cattle to the center of the field and send your dog past the cattle to achieve the stop with forward lateral pressure (diagrams 1 and 2). After they have achieved a stop, slowly proceed to your dog. This will create movement and reverse the parallel pressure (diagram 3). Send your dog forward again, recreating a stop. When that stop is achieved. Stand quietly, step back, and call your dog to return. Stepping back for a distance is important because it releases pressure. If the cows remain stopped and stand quietly, quit. If there is movement, recreate the stop again. When they are stopped and standing, quit. The quit, or the release, is as important as any effort we make. This initial effort of creating the stop will take several days. The reaction will be subtle. The reaction we want to see is when the cattle see us approach, they start grouping on their own.

With the stop achieved, we will try to create movement. A slow and steady quiet pressure, steady side-to-side action, or rocking motion will create movement and an opportunity to recreate the stop. After achieving movement and the ability to create the stop at any desired location, quit. The next step will be increasing the pressure to achieve a faster response, a flight or fleeing reaction from your cattle. This flight or fleeing is intended as a reaction from the group as a group. This simulates a predator's pressure. By creating flight, we can promote stress and pressure that we can use as a training opportunity to promote the stop and the *standing solution* (diagram 1). This can be accomplished by trotting toward the cattle or from side to side, or if afoot, jumping up and down. Do not yell, hoop, or holler, or use any pressure to intensify a reaction of movement so that we can recreate the stop. Upon achievement of the flight and the stop, quit.

After achieving the desired response of the standing solution, the next step will be the effort to begin shedding or separating individuals (diagram 4). Encouraging individual flight is to simulate a more intense predator pressure. The goal is the separation from the herd where the individual receives pressure. The blocking of the return to the herd creates an understanding that the herd is where the individual can find security and safety. The release of the pressure is the return to the herd. This creates a calm resolve and is *predator awareness*. The goal is a routine persistent instinct to encourage this reaction from our cattle where their best response is the *standing solution* when any pressure or stressful situation evolves.

The goal of *predator awareness* is a divergent stance, where cattle are standing in different directions. This is a sign of nonmovement, and they should be standing calmly and show no signs of stress. This content resolve is *predator awareness*. This training is a change in procedures. We are creating herding instincts that when predators create pressure, our cattle stand. Removing the chase and interrupting the predator-prey relationship.

All classes of cattle need to respect the pressure and seek the calmness and safety of the herd. The difference in the type of group and their familiarity with canines will be the determining factor for the length of time it will take to sufficiently instill *predator awareness*. This is an ongoing endeavor that is a change in handling. These efforts should be dealt with the seriousness of any other ranch chore that is given its specific attention. As you would not schedule a branding when you have hay to bale, don't schedule other livestock tasks with *predator awareness* training. It will proceed into a daily routine, but in the beginning, give it the full attention it deserves.

When we achieve our objective of creating *predator awareness*, the flight zones become very small or nonexistent once the *standing solution* is established. Pressure points only establish grouping and a firmer stance. The cattle have sought the herd as a defensive position finding comfort and security with others. After establishing the *predator awareness* stance and its reaction, cattle become accustomed to the training and the desired reaction is instinctual. Without pressure, the cattle graze with *herd awareness* contently, until pressure creates the reaction of *predator awareness.*

Riding through cattle that do not react to your presence becomes the normal behavior until pressure is applied. A light pressure will show that the cattle are still trained with *predator awareness.* This is recognizable by a movement toward others and a stance as a herd (diagram 5). This is a training update that should be applied and practiced routinely. When normal moving of cattle with stock dogs occurs, the cattle will perceive pressure and apply the *standing solution.* Tight quiet control of stock dogs is required or not using them at all.

In Northern California, there are many alfalfa fields that interface with juniper studded foothills. The deer often come in for their share of the crop. The deer graze in a herd and are undisturbed until they receive pressure. Upon pressure, they leave the field, following the lead. In history, it has had many names—follow the leader, follow the follow, follow the draw, to name a few. This behavior is observed throughout nature by waterfowl, mammals, fish, and birds—they all follow. The movement of the cattle can be treated the same way. The *lead* in this situation is an invisible tow line or a leash connection between the *lead* rider and the herd.

Using the *lead* cow that knows just where she is going encourages her to be herd bound. Working in pairs, one person can become the leader while the dog and other person create the parallel pressure to herd and move the cows (Gill, Machen). Reverse parallel pressure will create movement in the opposite direction (diagram 3). Also, remember that forward parallel will slow or stop movement (diagram 2). Starting the cattle with lateral pressure and then riding in the reverse parallel or opposite of the traveling direction will create movement in the desired direction. The nonlead rider will fall in and proceed behind the cattle while the *lead* will loop wide and move in the direction the cattle are moving. When passing the cattle, be outside of the flight zone and proceed forward at a trot or extended trot. Do not run. This will allow the leader to lead, and movement must continue or the cattle will stop. By using a calm call or song, the cattle will soon adopt the lead rider as their leader and follow nicely to the destination (diagram 6).

Like a rubber band, too much stretching, or distance, in this case, will cause the connection between the lead and the cattle to be broken, though too short of a distance and the *lead* will block and signal a *standing solution* in the herd. Proper distance for the *lead* rider is determined by the situation, type of stock being led, and the terrain being traveled. For example, when gathering yearlings in open flat to moderately hilly country, the lead may be a hundred yards up to a quarter mile in front of the stock. Mother cows in the mountains with a twisty trail will be closer from twenty to fifty yards. With a repetitive call or song, the leader creates a connection with the livestock. Repetition in this helps the tow line and strengthens it. The volume should be a connection between the *lead* and the stock in tow. If too loud, it acts as hooping and hollering and deters the lead acts and alerts possible predators who may become curious and follow. Too low and soft and the connection will be missing. If the lead connection is broken, it may be repaired by returning and leading again. It may be possible to start the reverse parallel pressure to recreate the movement, then looping forward to reinstate the connection. It could also be as simple as eye contact and calling calmly. This is something that will be behavior learned with time and practice.

The speed to travel is determined by the stock being led. Yearlings on the flats will have a faster pace than cows on a mountain trail. The cattle set the pace, and the lead has to match their speed while maintaining the connection. While maintaining the connection, the lead needs to be aware of the surroundings looking at the terrain for complications, watching the cattle for exhaustion or thirst. Gates are an obstacle to all operations. As the *lead* arrives at the gate, stop and stand, creating a *standing solution*, until the tail of the herd is in that group. Then open the gate and walk on. If the tow line is intact, proceed. If the connection is broken, repair it. Moving the herd, the mindset needs to be "the objective and the goal, not the procedure and its duration." Remember to avoid tight time lines. By using the *lead* approach, we stop driving cattle. Driving cattle disconnects our efforts from creating *herd awareness*, and the action of driving cattle away only strengthens the reaction of fleeing and the *chase*. We want to eliminate that predatory response and promote *herd awareness*. The lead is a solution to the problem of moving predator-aware cattle. It is a versatile way of moving cattle in general, but it is not necessary for cattle that are not conditioned with the *standing solution*. Cattle that have received *predator awareness* training and are confident in the *standing solution* are easily started and proceed nicely with the reverse parallel pressure and then rear pressure. Connecting with a *lead* only establishes the direction to proceed in calmly and quietly. If the cattle have been exposed to a predator and were not equipped with *predator awareness* training and they will not drive, the best approach is to lead them.

One concern is that the cattle that are exposed to predators are highly excited and aggressive toward stock dogs, making them difficult to move (J. Williams, D. E. Johnson, P. E. Clark, L. L. Larson, and T. J. Roland). These cattle have learned *predator awareness* the hard way. If they are educated by predators, and they will be, then our pressures are equal to the predators. Human presence relays fear and stress, making handling a rough and challenging situation. But if *predator awareness* is established, then the stress is released, and movement is something that they have already experienced in training.

By creating the solution of how cattle should react when presented with conflict, their behavior becomes one of calm fortitude and providing a secure place to oppose an apex predator's presence. Presented and taught by the ranchers themselves, we are removing the fear and stress that is associated with the pressure of the chase while realizing that predators exist and cattle have a risk of contact. These efforts we make to improve our management practices create a solution that ranchers can instill into their livestock operations with a practice of *stockmanship*. That will add to the bottom line and create a positive approach in a very hostile and costly environment.

Pictured above, CON cows have not been exposed to wolves. WLF cows have been exposed to wolves. This is *predator awareness* the hard way. Studies of the stress related to simulated wolf encounters and the difference between cattle exposed to wolves and cattle that had no previous exposure have been completed (R. F. Cooke, B. I. Cappellozza, M. M. Rise, D. D. Johnson, M. M. Norman, J. Williams, and D. W. Bohnert).

In Northern California, the feed grounds offer an excellent risk and reward venue and is a very good location for training. There are different areas and time frames that can be used for training such as winter feeding or calving time although calving time has its separate but definite challenges. The key is anytime is appropriate for training as long as it is prior to turnout and exposure to an apex predator. The more time that can be practiced creating *predator awareness* is a value. It is not unusual to see cows standing at the gate, waiting to be fed and then mobbing the hay wagon. By applying pressure and moving the herd to the center of the field where they stand receiving *predator awareness* training, the *standing solution* becomes a calm, resolute herd, waiting patiently for the training to end and breakfast to begin. They have the reward of calm herd security. When they are released, they have the reward of the hay. What becomes prevalent after several training mornings instead of being at the gate, ready to mob the wagon, they are in the center of the field standing calmly as a herd, waiting to be fed, calmly, without mobbing the hay wagon, which has the benefits of less injuries to cows and calves.

As mentioned previously, calving time creates its own challenges. Cows prefer to leave the herd and find a nesting and birthing spot that they find comforting, individualizing themselves from the herd. This seclusion is instinctual, not a time to be training *herd awareness*, but a time when monitoring predator's presence could be considered good management. Pairs, cows with a baby or young calf, can provide an effective training opportunity. It will help to understand which cows are at risk of individualizing themselves and being vulnerable to a predator, as well as leaving their calf as the second course of a predator's meal. The desirable response from the cow is to tighten to her calf and stand firmly or move and seek other cattle with her calf. The pressure on the pair must be soft in the beginning, and after several attempts should have the pair seeking the herd and the herd's comfort and security. A cow's response to a predator's pressure should be to seek others, stand firm, and react as *musk ox* or *bison* and deter predation. The key that we are seeking is a group standing calmly in a divergent pattern.

We deal with several predators, but the management of some predators has parameters set by law. Most ranches have rotational and seasonal grazing areas and calving times that coordinate the feed and its availability and the local weather. Calving dates are set in stone for most ranches and cannot be altered. Sometimes calving areas can be moved, but often, that is cost-prohibitive. The economic structure of each ranch and geographic parameters have established deadlines and dates that each operation must adhere to for financial sustainability.

Other effective predator management solutions can be used, but they also have costs and challenges. Human presence will deter most predators. Twenty-four seven monitoring, or patrolling, is not a realistic solution. But daily monitoring of the edges of the calving area and scenting are realistic options. The fear of humans is strong in most predators, and that fear can be used to our advantage. When using the scenting approach, frequently change the locations of the scent, around once a week, and be careful not to overdo applications or repeat the use of specific scents. All the scents related to humans, such as colognes, deodorants, soap, and cleaners need a light approach. More is not better in this case, and do not repeat the same scent for several weeks. Some good scenting items are an old farmer's ball cap that is destined for the trash, an unwashed tool that may be placed for a week, then moved to a new location. Just like attracting predators with scent for trapping or predators being attracted to boneyards, scent can spook predators and deter their presence just as other scents attract.

During turnout, there is still the predator's presence. If training begins during this time, it will be challenging but doable. When teaching *predator awareness* on an open range, one of the greatest challenges is the expansive area and the cattle distribution and the distance between individuals and others. It must be understood we are *stopping* cattle and holding them, but the chance of getting the same cattle for a repeat session may not exist for a period. So the effort to establish *herd awareness* draws out to a more intensive session. After achieving the *standing solution*, we leave, hopefully to locate our next group and then return later to visit the first group. Upon our return, success is seen when their reaction is grouping with their *herd awareness*. We spend a little more time encouraging predator awareness and then return to the second group only to repeat the first group's training. Each group would be of a different number of animals, but it would be ideal for each group to be about six to ten pairs. This training venue will take much more effort than training in other locations. But the positive side is that human presence is established, fulfilling the *predator awareness* training and the range rider task (Antonelli, et al. 2016).

Training *predator awareness* here is better spent using other deterrent practices on open ranges and large pastures. Mentioned above was the practice of scenting. All the suggestions apply to open range, but the distances require more product. There is still a need to change scents or items frequently, and the rule of more is not better still applies. There have been many talks and opposition to *range riders*. It is as effective as the riders are capable. Their understanding of the range or pasture is key, as well as its geography, climate, operations of the area, livestock awareness, and handling capabilities. All these work well with the continued management efforts and the task of instilling herd reaction and practicing *predator awareness*. Although *range riders* have had positive results, the cost factor is a downside. The *range rider* costs are high—to hire a person to an area of the operation that has never required a laborer before takes most operations backward. Another deterrent that has been mentioned, although an unproven hypothesis, is belling the cattle. There is more research that is needed to accredit that scenario, but investigations seem to support the conclusion that belled cattle are less likely to be at risk.

Risk assessments are a useful management tool for understanding predator behavior and mitigating predatory risk. A *risk assessment* is an evaluation of a producer's operation and its dynamics along with the predatory risks that may be there now or in the future. Predatory behavior, habitat, geography, and production risks are all evaluated, and a summary is presented. With the identification of predatory risks, a suggested plan can be worked out between the rancher and the assessment service provider, a *proactive stewardship* solution. There are those though that wish to participate in *proactive stewardship* and share in the costs associated with those practices. Although the practice has economic benefits, it is a challenge for us ranchers to change and operate outside our ranches' traditional parameters, but *proactive stewardship* has its rewards. Recommendations to mitigate risk through legal proactive measures are the objective of a *risk assessment*. Choosing a risk assessment service should have some careful consideration. An ideal risk assessment service will have local industry awareness, knowledge of the predators, a thorough understanding of the geography, climate, and range conditions, as well as having strict confidentiality standards.

Since there are not many available management resources to prevent the wolf and livestock confrontation, it is important that actions don't jeopardize the efforts and allow our opponent, the wolf, to get the upper hand. Large pastures, open ranges, or areas that have predatory potential should not be the pasture that you send older, feeble, or crippled cows too. The larger the calf, the greater the independence that calf will have and will show an increased desire to be on its own. The individualizing and singling out is what this training is trying to prevent. Younger pairs have a tighter mother-to-calf bond and a better tighter grazing relationship. They may be a better choice for some areas that may have predatory potential. Also trying to prevent things that attract, such as boneyards, hunting aftermath, and noises such as weaning or separation and even yelling or hooping and hollering. If sick or distressed livestock is found, remove them, unless they are doctored at the location. Then make sure they are left with other livestock settled and content. While checking and riding open range, be aware of the environment and the surroundings, such as tracks, signs, and trails, not only looking at predators' existence but signs of cattle disturbance. Some things to look at would be their feces and their placement, their travel routes, and disposition. When riding, be attentive to your dogs. They will alert you to many signs, any canid, or a scrap of evidence. Their route or path often is where tracks will be found along with game trail intersections. Sounds and signs of birds can alert you to issues of concern. Be aware of drinking areas, cattle, and other tracks, and become familiar with roads and trails that cross or intersect with game trails.

One of the management solutions is human presence. In order for it to be effective, the *wolf* must fear man, and establishing contact with wolves only diminishes the wolves' fear. It is comparable to the "old saddle horse," safe and sound, and to recreate his bronc attitude of youth is not possible. Once the wolves' fear of humans is gone, his demeanor only becomes emboldened, making the effort to chase or harass him only substantiates that you can't pursue him far enough or pose any punishment effective enough to deter him from returning. It is unknown if wolves, like domestic canines, recognize individuals and their scents or if it is more broadly applied to all humans. In order to keep the fear of humans, we must stay mysterious and as elusive as the wolf is to us. Keeping his fear of humans in our management arsenal is key to human presence working as a deterrent. On a ranching operation, an effort to deter or discourage the wolves' presence by contact may only instill a bolder curiosity. Without the fear of the risks, it may only encourage the wolf to return. Our efforts as ranchers should focus on our livestock. Remember, *we do not chase wolves. We tend livestock.*

DIAGRAMS

Diagram 1: The Stop

The stop is the basis for creating "the standing solution" and achieving "predator awareness." By accomplishing the stop and encouraging flight and then stopping the cattle again, you are instilling herd awareness. With pressure and release, you are establishing that the herd is a calm and secure place.

1. The Stop

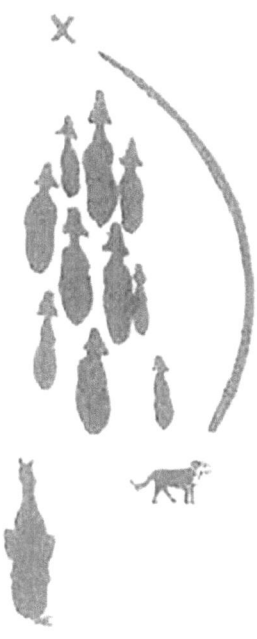

Diagram 2: Forward Parallel Pressure

Parallel pressure creates movement or removes it. Forward pressure acts as a brake, slowing or stopping movement. It is applied at the outside edge of the flight zone. The closer the pressure to the flight zone, the greater the brake. The further away from the flight zone only aids in slowing. Slightly further out has no effect and is considered the passing zone.

2. Forward Parallel Pressure

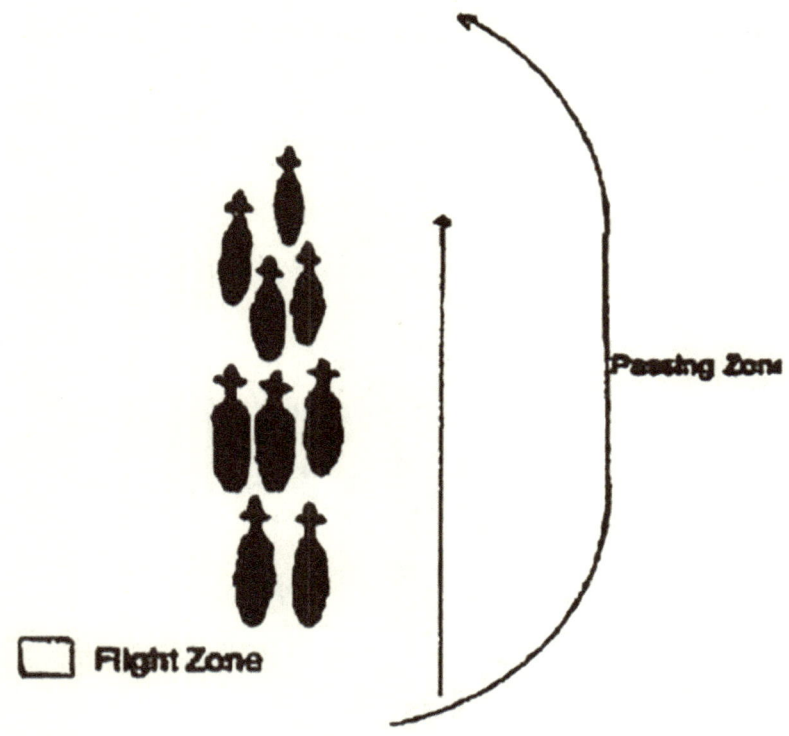

Passing Zone

Flight Zone

Diagram 3: Reverse Parallel Pressure

Reverse parallel pressure creates movement in the opposite direction the pressure is applied. The speed created is the proximity to the flight zone. The closer to the flight zone, the quicker the pace; the further out, the slower the pace.

3. Reverse Parallel Pressure

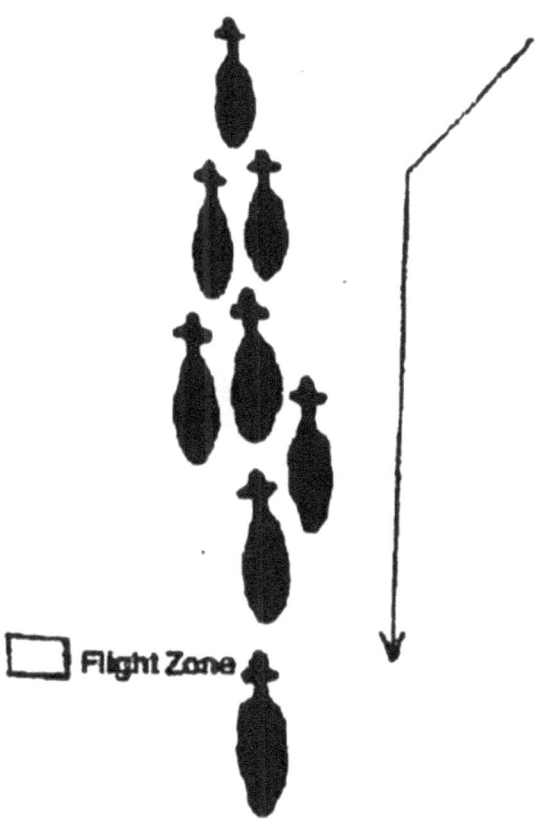

Diagram 4: The Block

By encouraging shedding and blocking the return, you are establishing that by being individualized, the cow receives pressure. The reason for the block is to establish the understanding and encourage the desire to return to the herd. The return when aloud is the relief of pressure, establishing the herd as a safe and calm place.

4. Shedding

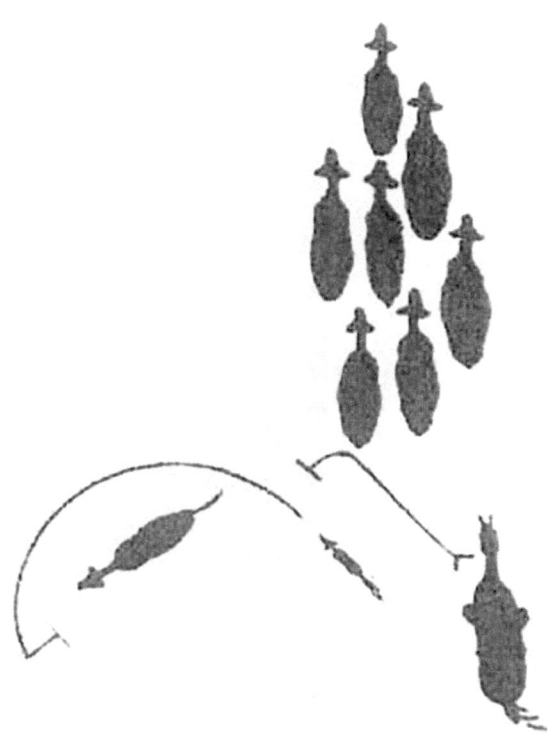

Diagram 5: Standing Solution

This is our goal, movement removed, divergent stance, with calm resolve.

5. Standing Solution

Diagram 6: The Lead

By establishing the standing solution, we are creating a herding instinct that creates changes in driving cattle (or a predator's pressure). They may drive and stand, drive and turn then stand. With the lead, we connect to the cattle and create a calm reaction of movement. With lateral pressure and then turning to reverse parallel pressure to create movement, then looping to the direction desired and establishing a visual and verbal connection, we can proceed to our desired destination.

GLOSSARY

Apex predator. A predator that is at the top of the food chain

Dry bred cows. Bred cows not lactating

Flight zone. An invisible perimeter area that when encroached upon creates movement

Heading dog. Stock dogs of any breed have instinctive approach bred into them. They will instinctively move to areas of a cow each time they challenge a cow. A head dog proceeds to the head of a cow.

Musk ox. A ruminant species of North America that defends against predators by grouping in a circle

Pairs. Mother cow with a nursing calf

Pressure point. An invisible perimeter area that a cow becomes aware of a presence, yours or others

Replacement heifers. Young females selected to become future cows

Weaned calves. Calves removed from mother cow to prevent nursing

Yearlings. Subadults

REFERENCES

Antonella, Sarah. 2016. "An Analysis of Wolf-Livestock Conflict Hotspots and Conflict Reduction strategies in Northern California."

Grandin, Temple, and Mark J. Deesing. 1998. "Genetics and Behavior during Handling, Restraint, and Herding." *Genetics and the Behavior of Domestic Animals.* 113–144

Mooring Michael S., and Benjamin L. Hart. "Animal Grouping for Protection Parasites: Selfish Herd and Encounter-Dilution Effects." *Behavior* 123.3 (1992): 173–193.

Oregon State University Beef Cattle Sciences. "Impact of Previous Exposed to Wolves on Temperament and Physiological Responses of Beef Cattle Following a Simulated Wolf Encounter."

R. F. Cooke, B. I. Cappellozza, M. M. Regis, D. D. Johnson, M.

M. Borman, J. Williams, and D. W. Bohnert. Oregon State University.

J. Williams, D. E. Johnson, P. E. Clark, L. L. Larson, and T. J. Roland. 2017. "Wolves—A Primer for Ranchers."

Ron Gill, PhD, Rick Machen. "Cattle Handling Points Stockmanship and Low-Stress Handling." Texas A&M.

COMMENTS AND OBSERVATIONS

Some of the comments that have been mentioned prior to the project's completion were that it was too large of a project to be effective. The actual training is basically a simple effort. Our livestock has a natural faded instinct of herding. The stockmanship approach and applied management practices will soon have our livestock reacting as herd groups, creating a proactive solution for predator livestock confrontation.

Through the efforts of training the *standing solution*, one of the observations has been how subtle the reactions become. Individual livestock awareness becomes more obvious in response to their surroundings and any movement within their increased awareness zone. Livestock heads come up and evaluate the risk. If the risk seems minimal, the heads go back down, and they resume eating. If the risk is stressful, they begin a movement toward others.

Prior to the *wolf's* presence and developing *predator awareness* training, our ranch historically had predatory losses, predominantly coyotes, but we have lost a few to lions also. What we have noticed for the last several years is no losses to any mammal predator.

> After the wolves have consumed all the natural prey, such as deer and elk, it will be extremely difficult to keep them from consuming livestock. Behavioral methods of controlling predation of livestock will be impossible if most of the natural prey has been eaten. (Temple Grandin)

Livestock often chooses the least difficult path. Predators also choose the path of least resistance. By creating cattle that have a resistance to pressure, *predator awareness*, the predator may just move on, choosing a less challenging opponent.

All deterrents are a challenge to measure whether they have been successful or not. The most successful action may be having a neighbor that does nothing.

A comment that has been posed to this method is the *wolf* will just learn to attack the herd. In the wild, there is not a predator that will attack an entire herd at once. That is reserved for *man*, and we call it *war*.

Special thanks to the USFWS, Yreka, California, https://www.fws.gov/yreka/.

ABOUT THE AUTHOR

Mark Coats is a lifelong rancher born in 1959, although he wasn't raised on a multigenerational ranch because his father left that ranch to fight in WWII and upon his return was discharged to San Diego, California. Mark's father fell in love with California and its climate and spent the rest of his life here.

His father never lost the desire of being involved in agricultural endeavors and passed that love on to Mark. Although a modest fiveacre ranchette, it afforded Mark many opportunities. At an early age, Mark was raising and selling pigs and sheep, as well as training and trading a few horses.

Mark's first ranching job at the age of thirteen was helping out at a purebred Charolais Ranch in Manteca, California. His obligations were tending a string of show cattle, as well as helping with general ranch work, which included almonds.

His second job was in Clovis, California. It was for another purebred outfit. The breed, though, happened to be Brahman. Mark's first cow owned was at the age of fifteen, and that cow was a registered Brahman.

The list of ranches Mark worked for continued, encompassing a lot of countries throughout the west. They included California, Nevada, and Oregon. Those experiences were on public lands or large ranches and from the back of a horse.

Mark's first ranch management job was at the age of twenty-one. It was the same year that he married his high school sweetheart. Their combined efforts have kept them active in the ranching business to this day.

In 2004, they purchased a ranch in Dorris, California, and left Oakdale, California, where they had made their home for nineteen years.

In 2011, the wolf passed through their ranch. Being active in the local Cattlemen's Association, as well as other community boards and advisory positions, Mark sought solutions to keep his ranching operation viable.

In 2015, Mark received a grant from the USFWS for writing a paper and producing a DVD for his deterring efforts of predator awareness. He has been published in quite a few newspapers and magazines, interviewed on radio, and been asked to speak at different events. In 2016, he started a website, www.rancherpredatorawareness. com.

The efforts of sharing these experiences and techniques is to inform the public that proactive stewardship may not fit into everyone's program, but it is an effective method in mitigating risk of predator versus livestock encounters.